S0-AWR-441

SPECTRUM WRITING

CONTENTS

Project Editor: Sandra Kelley
Text: Written by Mary Waugh
Design and Production by A Good Thing, Inc.
Illustrated by Karen Pietrobono, Claudia Fouse, Anne Stockwell,
Teresa Delgado, Doug Cushman

This book is dedicated to our children — Alyx, Nathan, Fred S., Dawn, Molly, Ellen, Rashaun, Brianna, Michele, Bradley, BriAnne, Kristie, Caroline, Dominic, Corey, Lindsey, Spencer, Morgan, Brooke, Cody, Sydney — and to all children who deserve a good education and who love to learn.

McGraw-Hill Consumer Products

Things To Remember About Writing

WRITING

- Use sentences in a paragraph only if they tell about the main idea of the paragraph.
- Use words like *next* and *yesterday* to tell when something happens.
- Write directions for doing something in proper order.
- Use *er* or *est, more* or *most* to compare things.
- Use details to tell how something looks, sounds, smells, tastes, or feels.
- Use names, places, and dates when writing facts. Use words like *think* and *should* when stating an opinion.
- Use words like *since* and *because* to join cause and effect parts of sentences.
- Think about your purpose before you start writing.
- Try writing about something from different points of view.

REVISING

- Use words that are exact to make your sentences clear.
- Be sure every sentence has a subject and a verb.
- Combine sentences to make your writing smoother.
- Make all verbs in a story tell about the same time.

PROOFREADING

Check to see that
- you used capital letters correctly
- you put in correct punctuation marks
- all words are spelled correctly
- you used correct verb forms

McGraw-Hill
Consumer Products

A Division of The McGraw-Hill Companies

Copyright © 1998 McGraw-Hill Consumer Products.
Published by McGraw-Hill Learning Materials, an imprint of McGraw-Hill Consumer Products.

Printed in the United States of America. All rights reserved. Except as permitted under the United States Copyright Act, no part of this publication may be reproduced or distributed in any form or by any means, or stored in a database retrieval system, without prior written permission from the publisher.

Send all inquiries to:
McGraw-Hill Consumer Products
250 Old Wilson Bridge Road
Worthington OH 43085

ISBN 1-57768-143-6

4 5 6 7 8 9 10 POH 03 02 01 00 99

unit 1
Writing Main Ideas

Things to Remember About
Using Main Ideas in Your Writing

The **main idea** of a paragraph is what the paragraph is about.

Writing

- Use sentences in a paragraph only if they tell about the main idea of the paragraph.
- Use a title as a short way to tell the main idea.

Revising

- Use more exact nouns to say just what you want.

Proofreading

Check to see that

- every sentence begins with a capital letter
- every sentence ends with a period
- all the words are spelled correctly
- every sentence has all the words it needs

Finding the right group

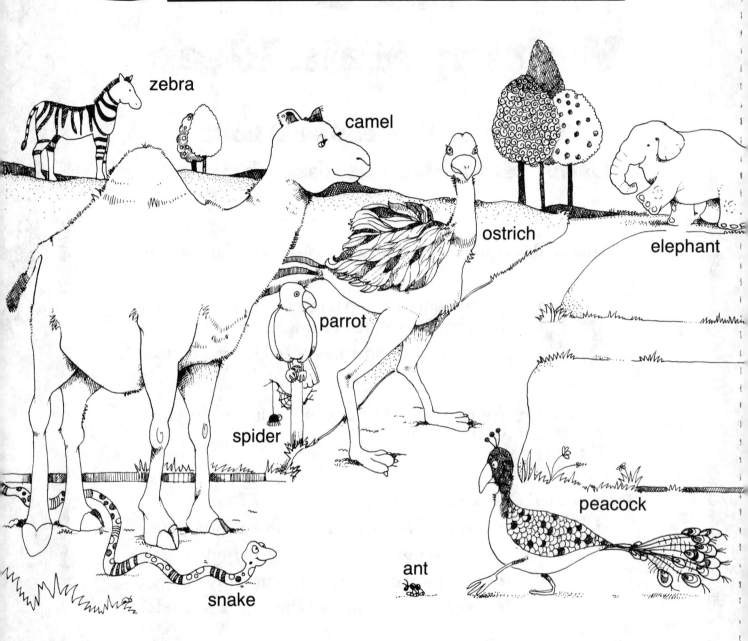

Pretend that you are a zoo keeper. You find your animals running all over. They are all mixed-up. How will you group them? Well, you can put each one in a **category.** A category is a group of things that are alike.

A. Read the category names below. Then write the name of each animal under the correct category name.

Animals with Four Legs	Animals That Crawl	Animals with Feathers

B. The words in each list below belong to a category. Their category names are: Holidays, Fruits, Colors. Write the correct category name above each list.

grape	blue	Halloween
apple	yellow	Columbus Day
banana	red	Memorial Day
pear	green	Thanksgiving Day

C. Read each list of words below. Then draw a line through the word that does *not* belong in each category. Finally, write a correct category name above each list.

sister	lemonade	cheek
mother	cake	nose
brother	milk	foot
car	water	ear

Read the category names below. On a separate sheet of paper, copy the three category names. Then write two words or draw two pictures that belong under each category name.

Things with Wings   People   Things to Read

A category is a group of things that are alike.

2 Writing the main idea of a picture

Look at the picture. What is the picture about?

A picture can tell us many things. But most pictures tell us *one* **main idea.** The main idea is what the picture is all about. The main idea is what the whole picture means.

A. Which sentence below tells the main idea of the whole picture? Circle your answer.

1. Some girls and boys are playing volleyball.
2. Some girls have curly hair.
3. Some boys are playing volleyball.

B. Which sentence below tells the main idea of this picture?

1. Fred has a new job.
2. Fred's apron is white.
3. Fred is cooking hamburgers.

CHEESE BURGER
HAMBURGER
HOT DOGS 2-2

SODA - ORANGE
GRAPE JUICE

C. Draw a picture in the space below. Then write the main idea of your picture on the line.

The main idea of my picture is: _____

_____

On another sheet of paper, draw three more pictures. Then under each picture, write its main idea. You might want to use the ideas below. Or think up your own ideas for the pictures.

Something that
happens at school

Something that
happens at home

Something that
happens at play

The main idea of a picture is what the picture is all about.

3 Writing the main idea of a paragraph

Read the paragraph below.

Fish sleep in different ways. Some sleep in the sand. Some sleep on their sides. Others sleep on their tails. One fish sleeps while standing on its head!

You know that pictures have main ideas. Well, paragraphs have main ideas, too. The main idea of a paragraph is what the paragraph is all about.

A. Read the paragraph about fish again. Then underline the sentence below that tells its main idea.

1. Fish are lazy.
2. Fish sleep differently.
3. Some fish sleep in the sand.

Read the next paragraph.

I got up early. I jumped out of bed. Quickly, I washed and dressed. Then I ran down the stairs. I gulped down my breakfast. I couldn't wait to go on my first camping trip.

B. What is the main idea of the paragraph? Circle the best answer.

1. I rushed to go camping.
2. I ate a big breakfast.
3. I ran down the stairs.

C. Write your own paragraph on the lines below. Make your paragraph at least four sentences long. You can choose one of the ideas below. Or you can think up your own idea.

I love to go skiing.
One day, I got lost while shopping.

_____

_____

_____

_____

Now write a sentence on the line below that tells the main idea of your paragraph.

_____

 On another sheet of paper, write two paragraphs. Write one paragraph about something that truly happened. Write the other paragraph about something you can imagine might happen. Write "I imagine" above the make-believe paragraph. Write "This really happened" above the paragraph that is true. Then write the main idea of each paragraph below it. Here are some ideas you may want to use. Or you can think up your own ideas.

The last day of school   Building a tree house
The day I went sky diving   Finding a million dollars

The main idea of a paragraph is what the paragraph is all about.

Writing paragraphs that make sense

What doesn't make sense in this picture?

Did you ever read something that didn't make sense? Something that doesn't make sense can juggle your mind. It can mix you up. A picture should make sense. A paragraph should make sense, too. A paragraph makes sense if all its sentences tell about the main idea.

Read the next paragraph. Think about the main idea as you read.

Tulips are my favorite flowers. I love to see the red, yellow, pink, and orange flowers in rows. Tulips tell me that spring is here. We have to stand in rows at school.

A. Answer the following questions about the paragraph. Write your answers on the lines.

1. What is the main idea of the paragraph? _____

_____

2. Which sentence doesn't make sense in the paragraph?

_____

3. Why doesn't one sentence make sense in the paragraph?

_____

B. Read the next two paragraphs. Then write your answers on the lines below each one.

Our neighbor told us about her trip into space. She built a spaceship. Last night, she flew in it. She zoomed out of the garage. I took a trip to Disney World. She climbed into space. She flew past many planets. She landed home this morning.

1. The main idea is: _____
2. The sentence that doesn't make sense in the paragraph is:

_____

Tugboats are small boats used to move large ships. I'd like to sail a ship someday. A tugboat's engine is very powerful. The small boat can pull or push. It's fun to see tugboats moving big ships around.

3. The main idea is: _____
4. The sentence that doesn't make sense in this paragraph is:

_____

Write On

Use this main idea: "One day I put my shoes on the wrong feet." Or use your own main idea. Then, on a separate sheet of paper, write a paragraph using the main idea you have chosen. Remember: Use only sentences that belong with the main idea.

Sentences belong in a paragraph only if they tell about the main idea of the paragraph.

5 Writing a title

Look at the picture below.

A **title** is a name for a picture or story. It tells what the picture or story is all about. A title is a short way to tell the main idea of a picture or story.

A. Look at the picture again. Then read the titles below. Underline the title that best tells about the picture.

1. Monkey Is Star of Bike Day
2. Playing in the Park
3. Some People Don't Ride Bicycles

Read the next story.

First, Charlotte hit her toe when she jumped out of bed. Then she had no clean socks to wear. At breakfast she burned her toast. Then she spilled her juice on her homework. It was not a good beginning to Charlotte's day.

B. What title below best tells about the whole story? Underline your answer.

1. Charlotte's Day
2. The Burned Toast
3. A Bad Beginning for Charlotte

C. Read the next story. Think about its main idea. Then write a title for the story on the line below.

Have you ever seen a UFO? Some people think UFOs fly around. But nobody knows what they are. Nobody knows if they are real. Some people say they have seen UFOs. Other people say UFOs are a trick.

A good title for this story is: _____

On a separate sheet of paper, write your own story. Make it four or more sentences long. Then write a title for your story on the top line of your paper. You can use one of the ideas below. Or you can think up your own idea.

Man Wins Flapjack Contest
Girl Invents New Glue
Elephant Escapes from Zoo

A title is a short way to tell the main idea.

Revising

Writing nouns that are more exact

lesson 6

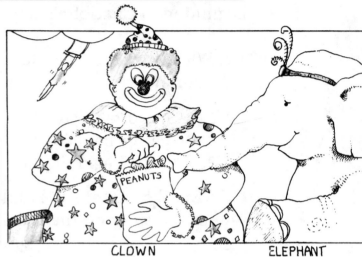

QUEEN   LION   CLOWN   ELEPHANT

The <u>person</u> fed the <u>animal</u>.

The sentence above tells about both pictures. But it doesn't tell enough. The nouns <u>person</u> and <u>animal</u> aren't very exact. The next sentence uses more exact nouns to tell about picture 1.

The queen fed the lion.

A. What more exact nouns would tell about picture 2? Write a sentence with more exact nouns for picture 2 on the line.

_____

B. Read the list of nouns below. Then write *two* nouns that are more exact next to the nouns given. The first one is done.

1. building _____*barn*_____ _____*house*_____

2. food _____ _____

3. toy _____ _____

4. flower _____ _____

12

C. Look at the picture. Read the nouns by each person, place or thing. Think of more exact nouns for each one. Using your more exact nouns, write three or more sentences about the picture on the lines below.

_____

_____

_____

_____

Look back at the sentences you've written for the **Write On** sections in this unit. Choose three sentences to rewrite. On another sheet of paper, rewrite the three sentences using more exact nouns.

Choose nouns carefully and they will say just what you want them to say.

Proofreading

Correcting your work

lesson 7

Study the story below.

> S.
> ~~S~~idney Hart   N
>   ~~n~~ovember 21,19___
>   T
>   Our Class ~~t~~rip
>   yesterday   went to
>   Our class trip was ~~yesterdy~~. We ~~go~~∧ the
>   model dinosaurs
> museum. We saw whale bones. We saw ~~modle dinisores~~.
>   monster   had
> We even saw footprints of a very old ~~monser~~. We∧ a
> great day.

The story has been **proofread.** Proofreading means reading over something you have written and then making corrections.

A. Write answers to the questions about the story on the lines below.

1. What mark is used to cross out one letter at a time? _____

2. What mark is used to cross out a whole word? _____

3. What mark is used to add a word? _____

B. Read the next story. Then, using the proofreading marks you have learned, write in the corrections that are needed. Think about capital letters, spelling, and missing words.

bert loves to rune. He sometimes all day long.

this yer he will on the school rack team.

14

C. Now write a paragraph on the lines below about a trip you took. The trip you write about can be one you took with your class or with your family or even by yourself. After you finish your paragraph, proofread it. Be sure to use the proofreading marks you have learned in this lesson.

_____

_____

_____

_____

_____

_____

_____

_____

Ask yourself these questions when proofreading your writing:

Does every sentence begin with a capital letter?
Does every sentence end with a period?
Are all the words spelled correctly?
Does every sentence have all the words it needs?

Post-Test

1. Cross out the words that do not belong under each category name.

Animals	Tools	Buildings
bear	hammer	tree
dog	butter	house
duck	saw	school
car	rake	barn

2. Read the next paragraph. Then underline the sentence below it that tells the paragraph's main idea.

   The last snows melted, and the buds on the trees became leaves. Songbirds returned just in time to see the first daffodils bloom. The whole world seemed new again.

   a. It takes a long time for snow to melt.
   b. Spring had begun.
   c. Birds fly south in winter.

3. Write a title for the next paragraph on the line below.

   _____

   The first bicycle had wooden wheels. Imagine how uncomfortable that would be! Wooden wheels did not absorb the bumps on roads like rubber wheels do. In fact, bicycles that had these wooden wheels were called "boneshakers."

4. Rewrite the sentence below. Make the underlined nouns more exact. Use your new sentence as the main idea of a paragraph. Write the paragraph on a separate sheet of paper.

   When I grow up, I will be a <u>person</u> and work in a <u>place</u>.

unit 2
Writing in Sequence

Things to Remember About Writing in Sequence

Sequence tells what comes first, next, or last.

Writing

- Use sequence words like *next* and *yesterday* to tell when something happens.
- Give directions in proper sequence when you tell how something is done.
- Write every story so that it has a beginning, a middle, and an end.

Revising

- Use exact verbs to make your sentences clearer and more interesting.

Proofreading

Check to see that you have
- begun special names with capital letters
- used a capital letter to write the word *I*
- begun every sentence with a capital letter

Writing picture stories

A. Look at the groups of pictures below. They can tell a story. Put each group of pictures in correct order so that they do tell a story. Write <u>first</u>, <u>next</u>, or <u>last</u> under each picture to show the correct order.

When you put each group of pictures above in order, you put them in **sequence.** Sequence tells you what comes first, next, or last.

B. The pictures below are in sequence. They tell part of a story. Finish the story by drawing the last picture in the space.

First

Next

Last

C. On each line below, write a sentence that tells about each picture in part **B.** Be sure that your sentences are in sequence.

First: _____

Next: _____

Last: _____

On another sheet of paper, draw your own picture story. Use at least three pictures for your story. Then write a sentence under each picture that tells about the picture. Be sure your pictures and sentences are in sequence. You can use the ideas below. Or you can think up your own idea.

Getting Splashed
Practicing a Music Lesson
Feeding Your Baby Sister

To tell a picture story, draw pictures in sequence.

2 Writing sequence words

Study the pictures above. The words that are underlined are **sequence words.** Sequence words tell when something happens. *First, then, next,* and *finally* are sequence words. Some other sequence words are *last, second, third, tomorrow, yesterday, before,* and *after.*

A. Read the lists of sequence words below. Then number each word to show which word tells first, second, or last. Use the numbers 1, 2, or 3.

___ middle   ___ night

___ beginning   ___ morning

___ end   ___ noon

B. Find the sequence words in the next paragraph. Underline each one.

First, I gave the crazy monkey a banana. Then she peeled it. Finally, she threw away the banana and ate the peel.

C. There are two groups of sequence words below. For each group, write three sentences in sequence using these words. One is done to show you how.

morning   afternoon   night

In the morning it was raining. That afternoon it began to hail. At night the snow started to pile up.

1.   yesterday   today   tomorrow

_____

_____

_____

2.   first   then   finally

_____

_____

_____

On another sheet of paper, write three sentences using the words <u>morning</u>, <u>noon</u>, and <u>night</u>. Have your sentences tell about something you do at these times of day. Be sure your sentences are written in sequence.

Use sequence words to tell when something happens.

3 Writing recipes

A **recipe** is a set of directions for making a kind of food. Read the recipe card below.

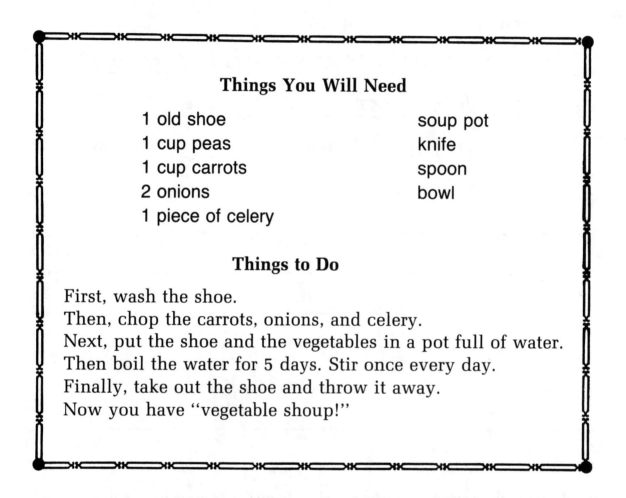

Things You Will Need

1 old shoe	soup pot
1 cup peas	knife
1 cup carrots	spoon
2 onions	bowl
1 piece of celery	

Things to Do

First, wash the shoe.
Then, chop the carrots, onions, and celery.
Next, put the shoe and the vegetables in a pot full of water.
Then boil the water for 5 days. Stir once every day.
Finally, take out the shoe and throw it away.
Now you have "vegetable shoup!"

A. That recipe may not taste very good, but it is written in sequence. What are the sequence words it uses? Write them on the lines below.

_____   _____   _____

_____   _____   _____

B. A recipe usually has two parts. The first part tells the <u>things you will need.</u> The second part tells the <u>things to do.</u> Read the words and sentences below. Then write the words or sentences on the recipe card that follows.

Egg Noodles

2 cups flour
First, break the eggs into
the flour.
3 tablespoons water
Finally, roll out the mixture.

Next, add the water and
salt and stir.
1 teaspoon salt
2 eggs

Things You Will Need

_____

_____

_____

_____

Things to Do

_____

_____

_____

 On another sheet of paper, write your own recipe. You can write a recipe for a cake or a stew, a pizza or a meatloaf. Or you may use your own idea. But be sure your directions are written in sequence.

When writing a recipe, give directions in sequence.

Writing "how to" directions

Look at the numbered dots below.

4
●

1
●

2
●

3
●

5
●

A. If you follow the directions below carefully, the dots will form a picture.

First, draw a straight line between dots 1 and 2. Then draw a line between dots 2 and 3. Next draw a line between dots 3 and 4. Then between 4 and 5. Finally, draw a line between 5 and 1. What picture have you drawn?

You already know what sequence means. You also know that a recipe is a set of directions that is written in sequence. Now you will learn how to write **how to** directions. "How to" directions tell just that, how to do something.

B. The following directions tell how to wash a car. But they are not in sequence. Put the directions in sequence by numbering each direction. Use the numbers 1, 2, 3, 4, 5, 6.

_____ Finally, dry the car with a soft, clean cloth.

_____ Second, fill the bucket with water and some soap powder.

_____ Fourth, wash the bottom of the car.

____ Fifth, rinse off the soap.

____ Third, wash the top of the car.

____ First, get a bucket, a hose, and a soft cloth.

C. Now, write your own set of directions for making a phone call. Use sequence words and write each step in sequence.

_____

_____

_____

_____

 On another sheet of paper, write one more set of "how to" directions. Make your directions at least 5 steps long. Remember to use sequence words and to write your directions in sequence. You can use one of the "how to" ideas below. Or you can think up your own.

How to build a skateboard
How to fly a kite
How to play your favorite game

"How to" directions tell how something can be done.
Write "how to" directions in sequence.

Writing story parts in order

Some stories are true. For example, most news stories are true. Most stories about real people's lives are true. Can you think of a story about a real person that is true?

Some stories are not true. They are about what a writer has imagined. They are make-believe. For example, *Cinderella* is a make-believe story. Can you think of another make-believe story?

Whether stories are true or make-believe, they all have a **beginning,** a **middle,** and an **end.** The beginning, middle, and end of a story are written in sequence. The beginning comes first, the middle comes second, and the ending comes last.

A. Read each story below. Then write <u>beginning</u>, <u>middle</u>, or <u>end</u> beside the correct part.

1. _____ Vera found a large egg.

   _____ A baby dinosaur hopped out of the egg.

   _____ She broke it.

2. _____ Next, a snake came out of the man's basket.

   _____ First, the man began to play his horn.

   _____ Finally, the snake began to sway to the music.

B. Each group of sentences below can tell a story. But one part of each story is not finished. Write the beginning, middle, or end of each story. Then write the word <u>beginning</u>, <u>middle</u> or <u>end</u> beside the part you have written.

1. It began to snow in the early evening.
    It snowed all night.

    In the morning _____

    _____

2. Jamie and I built a large boat.

    We _____

    _____

    Then we landed on a small island with strange animals.

3. The mailman _____

    _____

    I opened the package as quickly as I could.
    I found a sweater with my name on it.

On another sheet of paper, write a story that tells about the funniest thing that ever happened to you. Be sure your story has a beginning, a middle, and an end. Your story can be make-believe or true.

Write every story so that it has a beginning, a middle, and an end.

Revising

Writing with interesting verbs

The canoe <u>tipped</u>, and the boy <u>fell</u> into the water.

The words that are underlined in the sentence above are called **verbs.** Verbs tell action or help make a statement in other ways. If you choose exact verbs, they will help you say just what you want to say.

A. Read the sentences below. Then underline each verb.

1. Jan danced on the stage.
2. A frog jumped into my soup.
3. The squirrel scurried up the tree.

B. The most exact verbs make the most interesting sentences. Read the list of verbs below. Then write two verbs that are more exact next to the verbs given. The first one is done to show you how.

1. ran   <u>Sprinted</u>   <u>raced</u>

2. walked   _____   _____

3. ate   _____   _____

4. talked   _____   _____

C. Look at the picture below. There is lots of action. On the lines below it, tell what is happening in the picture. Use exact verbs to make your sentences interesting.

_____

_____

_____

_____

_____

Look back at the sentences you've written for the **Write On** sections in this unit. Choose five sentences to rewrite. On another sheet of paper, rewrite the five sentences using more interesting verbs.

Verbs tell action or help make a statement. Use exact verbs to make your writing interesting.

Proofreading

Using capital letters correctly

Jerry Holmes   September 25, 19___

My Green Friend

My friend is a praying mantis. He is mostly green. He sits very still. He loves to eat other insects. His favorite foods are flies and gnats.

Sometimes he eats out of my hand. He also likes to be petted. Often, I tie him to my bed. He looks out for bugs at night. He is a great pet.

Study the model story above.

A. Read the questions below. Then write answers to the questions on the lines.

1. With what kind of letter, a small letter or a capital letter, does each sentence begin? _____

2. How is the word I written? _____

3. What letters in the person's name who wrote this story are capitals?

   _____

4. How does the date begin? _____

   Study the box on the next page. It shows you special names that begin with capital letters.

People	Cities
Ms. Carla Jackson	Chicago
Mr. Peter Sanchez	Durham

Days	Schools
Tuesday	Washington School
Friday	East Central School

States	Holidays
New Mexico	Memorial Day
Pennsylvania	Thanksgiving Day

Streets	Months
Green Street	June
Oak Street	February

B. Now, using capital letters correctly, rewrite the paragraph below on the lines. Use the rules below to help you.

michelle myers goes to east windsor school. she jogs down spring street and sprints over to vine street. every wednesday she has soccer practice. on those days, she rides over to stanleyville.

_____

_____

_____

_____

_____

Begin special names with capital letters.
Use a capital letter to write the word I.
Begin every sentence with a capital letter.

Post-Test

1. Number the following words in sequence. Use the numerals 1–3 for each group.

   a. _____ tomorrow _____ yesterday _____ today

   b. _____ later _____ now _____ before

2. Write three directions that tell how you get to a friend's house from home. Use complete sentences and sequence words.

   a. _____

   b. _____

   c. _____

3. Write a more exact verb for each verb listed below.

   a. move _____   c. throw _____

   b. hit _____   d. laugh _____

4. Write capital letters where they belong in these sentences.

   a. next monday is columbus day, and lafayette school is closed.

   b. last may ellen gray and i flew to houston, texas.

5. Write a paragraph that tells what you plan to do after school today. Name at least four things you will do. Use sequence words to list these activities in the order you will do them. Try to use exact verbs in your sentences.

unit 3
Writing Comparisons

Things to Remember About Writing Comparisons

A **comparison** tells how things are alike or different.

Writing

- Add *er* or *more* to comparing words when you compare two things.
- Add *est* or *most* to comparing words when you compare more than two things.
- Use *better* and *best* when comparing *good*. Use *worse* and *worst* when comparing *bad*.
- Compare things by using *like* or *as* to make your writing more interesting.

Revising

- Use adjectives to make the meaning of your sentences clear.

Proofreading

Check to see that you have
- used a period to end a statement
- used a period to end a command
- used a question mark to end a sentence that asks something
- used an exclamation point after a word or sentence that tells strong feeling

Writing comparisons of pictures

When we **compare** things, we tell how they are alike or how they are different. The sentences beside the pictures are **comparisons**.

A. Study the pictures. Then read the comparisons. Finally, underline the comparisons that best tell about the pictures.

1.     One player is taller.
One player is thinner.

2.     One animal is longer.
One animal is smarter.

3.     The boy and girl are the same height.
The boy is in the fifth grade.

B. Using the pictures on the right side of the following page, write your own comparisons. Use the words at the top of page 35 for help. Make sure your comparisons are complete sentences. One is done to show you how.

Words used in Comparisons

more	fewer	louder
less	faster	same
bigger	higher	

1. The man on the left has bigger muscles.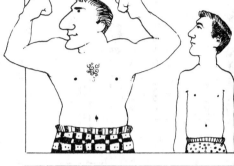

2. _____

3. _____

 On another sheet of paper, draw two sets of pictures. Draw the pictures in each set so that you can write comparisons for them. Then write a comparison for each set. Be sure to write your comparisons in complete sentences.

A comparison tells how things are alike or different.

2 Writing comparisons with er and more

Miff   Thor

Miff is <u>smaller</u> than Thor.   Thor is <u>larger</u> than Miff.

Both sentences above are comparisons. You already know that comparisons tell how things are alike or different. Well, some comparing words add **er** to their ends to make comparisons. For example: small, small<u>er</u> — tall, tall<u>er</u> — high, high<u>er</u>.

Now read the next sentence.

A feather bed is **more comfortable** than a bed of nails.

What are the words that make the comparison in that sentence? Words like *comfortable* use the word **more** to make comparisons. In fact, most long words use the word <u>more</u> to make certain comparisons. For example: beautiful, <u>more</u> beautiful — important, <u>more</u> important — dangerous, <u>more</u> dangerous.

A. Think about what you have learned. Then, using the list of comparing words, write two comparisons for the picture at the top of page 37. Add <u>er</u> to the correct words.

small   fancy   new   long   short

_____

_____

_____

B. This time write two comparisons using the word <u>more</u>. You can use the comparing words below. Or think up your own. Be sure to write complete sentences.

comfortable dangerous wonderful
exciting   beautiful   active

_____

_____

_____

 On a separate sheet of paper, write a story about a trip you might take. Use comparing words that have <u>er</u> endings or that use the word <u>more.</u>

 Below are some comparing words you may want to use in your story. Or you may think up other comparing words.

high   big   large   beautiful
short   fast   tired   dangerous

_____

Add <u>er</u> to short comparing words when you are comparing two things.
Use the word <u>more</u> with longer comparing words when you are comparing two things.

_____

3 Writing comparisons with est and most

Read the next paragraph.

Flora is the clever**est** magician I know. She can do the **most** wonderful tricks. Her new**est** trick is to make herself disappear. Too bad she hasn't learned how to make herself appear again!

Cleverest, newest, and *most wonderful* are all forms of comparisons. They compare more than two things. When comparing more than two things, add **est** to the ends of short comparing words. But use the word **most** before longer comparing words.

A. Read the following comparing words. Write the word <u>two</u> beside those that can compare two things. Write the words <u>more than two</u> beside those that can compare more than two things.

1. greatest _____

2. greater _____

3. most wonderful _____

B. Write a comparison sentence for each comparing word below. Write each comparison so that it compares more than two things. The two forms are done to show you how.

thoughtful *Harry is the most thoughtful person I know.*

great *That was the greatest time of my life.*

1. old _____

2. delicious _____

3. tall _____

Some comparing words drop, add, or change letters when they change form. For example: funny, funn**ier**, funn**iest**—large, larg**er**, larg**est**. If you are not sure of the spelling, check your dictionary.

C. Write three comparisons for the picture below. You may use the following comparing words or think up your own: <u>large</u>, <u>big</u>, <u>small</u>, <u>little</u>. Be sure to check your spelling.

1. _____

2. _____

3. _____

 Pretend you are the judge at a costume party. You have to choose the funniest costume, the ugliest costume, and the most unusual costume. On a separate sheet of paper, write a paragraph of five or more sentences that will tell about the costumes. Be sure to use the correct form for each comparison you write.

Add <u>est</u> to short comparing words when you are comparing more than two things.
Use the word <u>most</u> with longer comparing words when you are comparing more than two things.

Writing comparisons with good and bad

Read the sentences below that tell about the picture.

Sam has a **good** seat.
Felicia has a **better** seat than Sam.
Yolanda has the **best** seat of the three.

Now read the sentences below.

Marybeth's bike is in **bad** shape.
Nazir's bike is in **worse** shape than Marybeth's.
Frank's bike is in the **worst** shape of the three.

A. Read the sentences above again. Then answer the following questions. Write your answers on the lines.

1. What word compares two seats? _____

2. What word compares more than two seats? _____

40

3. What word compares two bikes? _____

4. What word compares more than two bikes? _____

B. Using the two forms of *good* and *bad* that you have learned, write your own comparisons on the lines below. The examples below will show you how.

Good
good   John is a good singer.
better   Manny is a better singer than John.
best   Estella is the best singer of the three.

Bad
bad   Angela has a bad cold.
worse   Glen has a worse cold than Angela.
worst   Melinda has the worst cold of the three.

1. good _____

2. better _____

3. best _____

4. bad _____

5. worse _____

6. worst _____

Now write about something you saw or something that happened to you. Using a comparison of <u>good</u> or <u>bad</u>, write at least one paragraph. You may use the ideas below or you may think up your own.

The Best Day At School   The Worst Storm

When comparing <u>good</u>, use the words <u>better</u> and <u>best</u>.
When comparing <u>bad</u>, use the words <u>worse</u> and <u>worst</u>.

---

5 Writing comparisons with like and as

Look at the picture. Then read the sentences below that tell about it.

My horse runs **like the wind.**
My horse runs **as fast as the wind**.

Another way to compare things is to use the words **like** or **as**. When used in comparisons, the words *like* and *as* tell how things compare.

A. Read the sentences about the picture again. Then write answers to the following questions on the lines.

1. To what are the sentences comparing the way the horse

   runs? _____

2. How many things are being compared in the first sentence?

   _____

3. How many things are being compared in the second sentence? _____

B. Read the following comparisons. Then write your own comparisons by finishing the phrases below.

Daria's smile is like a slice of watermelon.
She is as thin as a wrinkle.

1. Chico laughs like _____

_____

2. Our car is like _____

_____

3. The pudding looks like _____

_____

Write On Think about a summer day, a party, a friend, or your home. Or you may think about an idea of your own. Then on another sheet of paper, write at least one paragraph that tells about the idea you have chosen. In your paragraph, write comparisons that use the words <u>like</u> and <u>as</u>.

Below are the beginnings of some comparisons you may want to use. Or you may think up your own.

as soft as   the day was like
as lonely as   the food tasted like
as cheerful as   the room was like a

You can compare things by using the words <u>like</u> or <u>as</u>.

43

Revising
Writing with interesting adjectives

lesson

6

The plane is taking off.

The sentence above tells something about the picture. But it doesn't tell much. It would tell more if it used comparing words. You already know that comparing words tell how things are alike or different. A shorter name for comparing words is **adjectives.**

A. Now read the two sentences below that use adjectives to tell more about the picture above. Then underline the adjectives in each sentence.

1.   The huge, bright, new plane is taking off.
2.   The tiny, clumsy, old plane is taking off.

44

B. Underline each adjective in the next group of sentences.

1. Daisy got a shiny blue bicycle for her birthday.
2. It had a large basket on the handlebars.
3. Last week she took her fluffy kitten for a ride.
4. First, Daisy wrapped the kitten in a soft, green blanket.

C. Now write your own adjectives that tell about each noun below. Two are done for you.

_____old_____ house   _____new_____ socks

1. _____ rug   6. _____ magician

2. _____ hair   7. _____ elephant

3. _____ sky   8. _____ plant

4. _____ cat   9. _____ soup

5. _____ shirt   10. _____ glass

 Write a paragraph using one of the ideas below. Or you may think up your own idea. Make sure that your paragraph has at least one adjective in every sentence. You may use the list of adjectives below for help. Or you may want to think of your own adjectives.

Ideas	**Adjectives**		
Your favorite TV show	tiny	grumpy	heavy
Moving	old	swift	little
Your favorite person	huge	great	strange
Watching people	chilly	warm	beautiful
Flying in a plane	wonderful	slight	happy

Use adjectives to make your writing interesting.

Proofreading

Writing end punctuation

Read the following sentences. Notice how the **punctuation** is used.

Statement — He gave Erica a bunch of flowers.
Command — Pick up that pile of trash.
Question — How far is it to Okefenokee?
Exclamation — Yipe! That looks like a ghost!

period

•

A. Now write answers to the questions below.

1. What punctuation mark ends the statement?

_____

exclamation
point

2. What punctuation mark ends the command?

_____

3. What punctuation mark ends the question?

_____

question
mark

?

4. What punctuation mark ends the exclamation?

_____

B. Read the following sentences. Then write the correct punctuation mark for each one.

1. How long is that boat ____

2. Finish painting the fence by tomorrow ____

3. Mr. Hernandez took us to the zoo ____

4. Wow ____ Look at that hit ____

5. Where are you going ____

6. There is a crowd outside the palace ____

7. Don't push ____

8. Will the king give a speech ____

C. Now write the four kinds of sentences yourself. Write two statements, two commands, two questions, and one exclamation. Be sure to punctuate them correctly.

Statement — _____

Statement — _____

Command — _____

Command — _____

Question — _____

Question — _____

Exclamation — _____

Use a period to end a statement.
Use a period to end a command.
Use a question mark to end a sentence that asks something.
Use an exclamation point after a word or sentence that tells strong feeling.

Post-Test

1. Read the adjectives below. For each adjective, write the form that compares two things. Then write the form that compares more than two things.

   a. soft _____ _____

   b. sweet _____ _____

   c. interesting _____ _____

   d. exciting _____ _____

2. Write a comparing form of *good* to complete each sentence.

   a. Jeremy is a _____ runner than Kurt.

   b. Sarah is the _____ runner in the school.

   Write a comparing form of *bad* to complete each sentence.

   c. The burnt eggs tasted _____ than the burnt toast.

   d. The burnt oatmeal tasted the _____ of the three foods.

3. Complete the comparisons below.

   a. Dr. Bellows had a voice like a _____.

   b. The painting was as colorful as _____.

4. Write an adjective for each noun in the titles below. Then write a story, using one of the titles. Make your story at least four sentences long. Use at least one adjective in each sentence.

   a. The _____ Bear and the _____ Hunter

   b. _____ Children in a _____ House

   c. A _____ Day in the _____ Jungle

unit 4
Writing Details

Things to Remember About Writing with Details

Details are small parts that make a whole.

Writing

Tips

- Use details that tell about how something looks, sounds, smells, tastes, and feels.
- Use adjectives to describe objects and people.

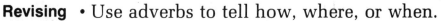

Revising

Tips

- Use adverbs to tell how, where, or when.

Proofreading

Tips

Check to see that you have

- used the s-form of the verb for certain singular subjects
- used the plain form of the verb for certain plural subjects

Writing details from pictures

Look carefully at the pictures.

The picture on the right has more **details**. Details are small parts that go together to make a whole. For example, one detail of the picture on the right is the book on the table.

A. Read the sentences below that tell details about the pictures. Then write the letter <u>R</u> beside each sentence that tells about the picture on the right. Write the letter <u>L</u> beside each sentence that tells about the picture on the left.

_____ 1. An alarm clock is on the table by the bed.

_____ 2. There is no bedspread on the bed.

_____ 3. A dog is lying on the rug near the bed.

_____ 4. There are curtains on the window.

_____ 5. There is no picture on the wall over the bed.

B. A group of sentences that tells details about something is called a **description.** On the lines below, write a description of your classroom or a room in your home.

_____

_____

_____

_____

_____

A   B

 Look carefully at both pictures above. Think about all the details. Then, on another sheet of paper, write a detailed description of each clown. Write the letter <u>A</u> above your description of the clown on the left. Write the letter <u>B</u> above your description of the clown on the right.

Details are small parts that go together to make a whole.

2 Writing with your senses

Study the pictures below.

A. The five **senses** are <u>seeing</u>, <u>hearing</u>, <u>smell</u>, <u>taste</u>, and <u>touch</u>. Write answers to the following questions about the pictures.

1. What sense are the children in picture **A** using mainly?

_____

2. What senses are the children in picture **B** using mainly?

_____

You know that details are small parts of a larger whole. You know also that a description is a group of sentences that tells details about something. When you gather details, you use your senses. Sometimes you use just one sense or mainly one sense. Other times you may use all of your senses.

B. Below is a description that uses four of the senses. Read the description. Then write the name of the thing being described.

It is round and red. It feels smooth. It tastes sweet. It sounds

crunchy when you bite it. It is an_____.

Think about a place you like to be. Or you may choose one of the places listed below. Then do the following things: First, write the senses <u>see</u>, <u>hear</u>, <u>smell</u>, <u>touch</u>, and <u>taste</u> across the top of another sheet of paper. Next, write details that tell about the place you chose under each sense. Finally, write your details together in a complete description. Be sure to write your description in complete sentences. If you need help, read the description in part **B** again.

    your kitchen at holiday time
    a park in the spring
    your favorite store

Use your senses when you write a description.

3 Writing about an object

Some words always describe things. Words like *smooth*, *soft*, and *loud* are describing words. You already know a word that means a describing word. That word is *adjective*.

A. Look at the picture. Think about the cat. Then circle the adjectives below that describe the cat.

square	fluffy	soft	mad
black	wet	sad	furry

Now think of two more adjectives that describe the cat. Write those adjectives below.

1. _____ 2. _____

B. Write one sentence that describes the object in each picture on the next page. Try to use at least two adjectives in each sentence. Then underline your adjectives. One is done to show you how.

A <u>scary</u>, <u>square</u> picture is on the wall.

1. _____

2. _____

 On another sheet of paper, write the name of your favorite food, toy, and clothing. Next to each favorite thing, write three adjectives that describe it. Remember to think about your five senses. After you have written your adjectives, choose one of the things to describe. Finally, write four or more sentences that describe your favorite thing. You may use the adjectives below.

Adjectives

playful	speedy	noisy	cold	tasty
furry	quiet	brown	sharp	sweet
colorful	red	bright	soft	yummy

Adjectives can help you to describe objects.

Writing about a person

You know some words that describe objects. There are words that describe people too.

A. Write the word or word group from the list under the picture of the person it describes. Some words may not fit either person.

Words That Can Describe People

tall	curly hair	wearing glasses
short	long hair	flowered dress
thin	dark hair	light hair
freckles	short hair	long pants

_____   _____

_____   _____

_____   _____

_____   _____

B. Write four or more sentences that describe the picture above. Try to describe everything that the picture shows. Tell how the boy looks, how he is dressed, and how he feels.

_____

_____

_____

_____

_____

Think about one of your favorite people. Think about how that person looks and how he or she acts. Think about what that person does best. Think about why you like that person. Then, on a sheet of paper, write a paragraph that describes your favorite person. Make your paragraph at least five sentences long. Remember to use words that you learned in this lesson and in the lesson about adjectives.

Adjectives can help you to describe people.

Writing riddles

Read the story above. A story that asks a question in an unusual way and then gives a funny answer is called a **riddle.**

A. Read the following riddles. Notice how they describe things. Then write answers to them on the lines.

1. Once I was a golden ball floating in a clear sea with a white wall around me. But someone broke my wall, and I became

    breakfast. I am an _____.

2. We are hard and white. One set of us falls out, but another grows back. We help you to say hello and to enjoy your

    Thanksgiving turkey. We are _____.

B. Look at the pictures below. Then think of a riddle that would describe each picture with only one detail. Write **X** next to the detail that would best help someone answer the riddle.

1.

___ I have four legs.

___ I bark.

___ I have a tail.

2.

___ People fly in me.

___ I am silver.

___ I have wings.

Now write some riddles of your own. On another sheet of paper, write at least three riddles. Think of animals, things to eat, things to wear, things in your home or classroom. After you have written your riddles, share them with the class or a friend. If you need help, look back at part **A** of this lesson.

Details are important in riddles.

Revising

Writing with adverbs

Read the next sentence.

The snake is crawling <u>quietly</u> <u>outside</u> <u>now</u>.

A. Now write answers to the questions below.

1. Which one of the underlined words tells how the snake is crawling? _____

2. Which word tells where the snake is crawling? _____

3. Which word tells when the snake is crawling? _____

Adverbs are words like those underlined above. Adverbs tell how, where, and when.

B. Find the adverbs in the sentences below. Underline each one.

1. I found my slipper outside today.
2. Rags was chewing it happily.
3. I yelled loudly, and he ran.
4. He ran upstairs and hid.
5. Later, I found him sleeping peacefully.

C. Now write adverbs to complete each sentence below. The words below the lines tell you which kind of adverb to write. One is done to show you how.

Laurie speaks _____ softly _____.
(how?)

1. Olivia found a skunk _____.
(where?)

2. Zeke got to school _____.
(when?)

3. The birds sing _____.
(how?)   (when?)

4. The children ran _____
(how?)   (where?)

_____.
(when?)

Look back over the sentences and paragraphs that you have written for this unit. Choose five sentences or one paragraph to rewrite. Rewrite your sentences or paragraph on another sheet of paper. Use at least one adverb for each sentence that you rewrite.

Adverbs tell how, where, or when.

Proofreading

Using the correct verb form

The pelican gulp**s** the fish.   The pelicans gulp the fish.

A. You already know that verbs tell action or help make statements in other ways. Write answers to the questions about the verbs in the sentences.

1. What are the verbs in the sentences below each picture?

_____   _____

2. How are the verbs different? _____

3. Which verb tells about more than one pelican? _____

Two verb forms are used with certain singular and plural subjects. If the subject is singular, like *pelican*, the verb has an *s* ending. If the subject is plural, like *pelicans*, the verb has no *s*.

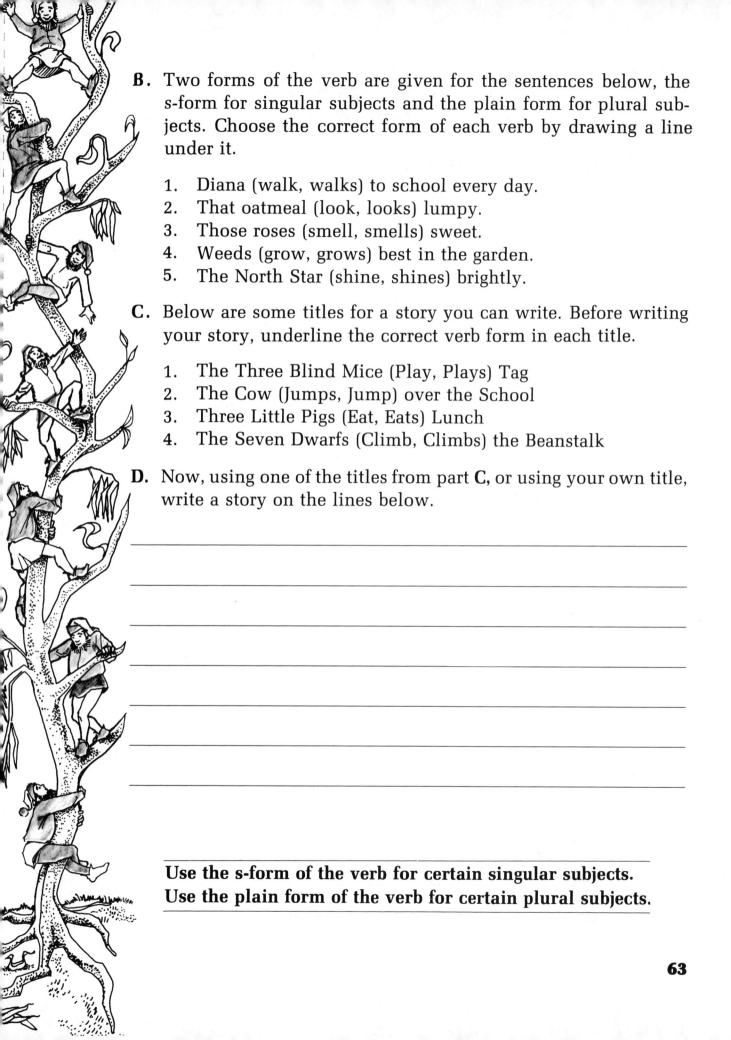

B. Two forms of the verb are given for the sentences below, the s-form for singular subjects and the plain form for plural subjects. Choose the correct form of each verb by drawing a line under it.

1. Diana (walk, walks) to school every day.
2. That oatmeal (look, looks) lumpy.
3. Those roses (smell, smells) sweet.
4. Weeds (grow, grows) best in the garden.
5. The North Star (shine, shines) brightly.

C. Below are some titles for a story you can write. Before writing your story, underline the correct verb form in each title.

1. The Three Blind Mice (Play, Plays) Tag
2. The Cow (Jumps, Jump) over the School
3. Three Little Pigs (Eat, Eats) Lunch
4. The Seven Dwarfs (Climb, Climbs) the Beanstalk

D. Now, using one of the titles from part **C,** or using your own title, write a story on the lines below.

_____

_____

_____

_____

_____

_____

Use the s-form of the verb for certain singular subjects.
Use the plain form of the verb for certain plural subjects.

Post-Test

1. Write four details about the picture below.

a. _____

b. _____

c. _____

d. _____

2. What does the following paragraph describe?

It has a head but cannot see or hear. It has a foot but cannot walk. It has many springs but no water. You use it every night and make it every day.

It is a _____.

3. Write two adjectives that describe a banana.

a. _____   b. _____

4. Look again at the picture above. Then complete the sentences below with adverbs.

a. The horse runs _____.

b. The men chase the horse _____.

5. Now write a paragraph that tells how the men catch the horse. Write at least four sentences. Use an adverb in each sentence.

unit **5**
Writing
Facts and Opinions

Things to Remember About Writing Facts and Opinions

A **fact** is something that is true. An **opinion** is what someone thinks or feels.

Writing
- Use names, places, and dates when writing facts.
- Use words like *think, feel, good,* and *should* when stating an opinion.

Revising
- Give every complete sentence both a subject and a verb.

Proofreading Check to see that you have
- spelled correctly those verbs that tell about something that has already happened

Writing sentences of fact and of opinion

A **fact** is a sentence that is true. An **opinion** is what someone thinks or feels. A sentence that is not true may tell about something that is *make-believe* or *false*.

Read the following sentences.

___ I go to school.

___ I think I would make a good astronaut.

___ I love blueberries.

___ I am an astronaut, and I travel to faraway places.

A. Now write <u>T</u> beside the sentence above that is true about you. Write <u>O</u> beside the sentences that tell what you might think or feel. Write <u>F</u> beside the sentence that is not true.

B. Read the sentences below. Then write <u>fact</u> beside the sentences that are facts. Write <u>opinion</u> beside the sentences that are opinions. Write <u>false</u> beside the sentences that are make-believe or not true.

1. _____Yesterday, I ate some food.

2. _____This morning I drove my family's car to school.

3. _____Some people think that winter is the best time of the year.

4. _____ The earth moves around the sun.

5. _____I will have to call a spaceship to get home today.

C. Now write two facts about a good friend. Then write one opinion about that friend. Make each fact and opinion a complete sentence.

Fact: _____

Fact: _____

Opinion: _____

_____

On another sheet of paper, write four sentences that tell about someone in your family. Make two of your sentences facts. Make the other two sentences opinions. Write <u>fact</u> next to the two sentences that tell facts. Write <u>opinion</u> next to the two sentences that tell opinions.

A fact is a sentence that is true.
An opinion tells what someone thinks or feels.

2 Writing about different topics

Look carefully at the picture below.

You know that facts are true, and opinions are what someone thinks or feels. Certain words are used to write opinions. You can use words like *think*, *better*, *worst*, *like*, and *should* when you write an opinion.

A. On the lines below, write two sentences that tell facts about the picture above. Then write two sentences that tell opinions about the picture. When writing facts, tell exactly what the picture shows. Use words like those above to show your opinion.

1. Fact: _____

2. Fact: _____

3. Opinion: _____

_____

4. Opinion: _____

_____

B. Now write some facts and opinions about your school. Some facts you might want to write are: where your school is, how many students go to your school, how old your school is, your principal's name, your teacher's name. Some opinions you might want to write are: if you enjoy school, what you like best about your school, what you don't like about your school, how you would change your school. Write your facts and opinions in complete sentences on the lines below.

Facts and Opinions About School:

1. Fact: _____

2. Fact: _____

3. Opinion: _____

_____

4. Opinion: _____

_____

Write On Think about your favorite book or story. Then, on a separate sheet of paper, write the name of the book or story. First, write two facts about it. One fact might be where you read or heard the story. Another fact might be the name of the person who wrote the book or told you the story. Next, write your opinion of the book or story. Make your opinion at least three sentences long.

Words like think, feel, best, and should are used to state an opinion.

3 Writing about yourself in a letter

Read the letter below carefully.

Date ————→

Greeting ————→

January 24, 19___

Dear Jane,

I'm glad you just moved into our neighborhood. I sure do enjoy meeting people my own age.

I'm 8 years old. I weigh 65 pounds and I am 4 feet tall. I have green eyes and blond hair. In the summer, I get millions of freckles. Well, maybe I don't get millions, but I do get a lot.

My favorite hobby is <u>spelunking</u>. Have you ever heard of spelunking? That's when you go looking for caves. I think spelunking is a good hobby because it's so exciting.

My favorite school subject is math. I enjoy math because it gives me a chance to figure out problems on my own. I also like math because it is easy for me.

Would you like to come to my house one day after school to play? I would like to know more about you. I'll talk to you about a visit when I see you in school next week. I hope we will become good friends.

Best wishes,
Donna

Closing ————→

Notice where the **date** of the model letter is placed. Look at the **greeting** and the **closing** of the letter. All letters in good form are set up this way.

A. Now read the letter again. Then underline every sentence in it that tells a fact. Circle every sentence in it that tells an opinion. Remember, opinions are what someone thinks or feels.

B. Write three or more facts about yourself on the lines below the word *Facts*. Write some of your opinions about yourself and other things on the lines below the word *Opinions*. Use complete sentences.

Facts

_____

_____

_____

Opinions

_____

_____

_____

 On a separate sheet of paper, write a letter to a person you have not seen in a long time. The person may be real or make-believe. Tell that person facts about yourself. Tell him or her some of your opinions.

Make sure your letter has both facts and opinions. Also, make sure your letter has the date, the greeting, and the closing in the correct form. If you need help, look back at the model letter and at part **B**.

You can write both facts and opinions in a letter.

4

Writing facts and opinions about animals

You know what facts and opinions are. Now you will write some facts and opinions about animals.

A. Read the names and look at the pictures of the animals below. Then, on the blank lines, write one or more facts about each animal. Be sure to write your facts in complete sentences.

A Bird   Facts: _____

_____

_____

_____

A Whale   Facts: _____

_____

_____

_____

A Mouse   Facts: _____

_____

_____

_____

B. Look at the picture of each animal below. Then write your opinion of each animal. You will probably use words like *best*, *think*, *like*, *bad*, and *feel* to show your opinion. Make sure your opinions are complete sentences.

A Dog

Opinion: _____

_____

_____

_____

_____

A Fish

Opinion: _____

_____

_____

_____

_____

Write On

On another sheet of paper, write a paragraph about an animal you would like to have as a pet. Make your paragraph at least five sentences long. Write both facts and opinions. Draw one line under your sentences with facts. Draw two lines under your sentences with opinions.

You can state both facts and opinions in a paragraph.

Writing a make-believe story

You know that some sentences can tell about things that are make-believe or not true. The next sentence tells about something that is make-believe.

Yin Shu chased the dragon.

Everyone knows that there are no real dragons. But make-believe is fun, and make-believe can help you write stories.

A. Read the sentences below. Then write **M** beside the sentences that tell about make-believe things. Write **F** beside the sentences that tell facts.

1. _____Our neighbor's dog told us a story yesterday.

2. _____Today Viola ate 94 hamburgers and 37 ice cream cones.

3. _____Once there was a girl who made candy canes out of red pencils.

4. _____Some people can stand on their heads.

Now read the following make-believe story.

Once there was a boy named Jack who had a cow. Jack lived with his mother way out in the country. They were very poor people.

One day Jack's mother told her son to go to town and sell the cow to get some money. Jack took the cow to town and sold it. But he didn't get any money for his cow. Instead he got *beans* for it. When Jack got home and told his mother what he had done, she became very angry. She snatched the beans out of Jack's hand and threw them out into the yard. Then she sent her son to bed without his dinner.

B. The story about Jack *could* be true. It has sentences that could be facts. But in this lesson you will write stories that tell about make-believe things. Write a make-believe ending to the story about Jack on the lines below. Make your ending at least five sentences long.

_____

_____

_____

_____

_____

_____

_____

 On another sheet of paper, write a complete make-believe story of your own. Be sure that you tell about something that is not real or not true. Make your story at least five sentences long. You may use one of the ideas below for your story or you may think up your own idea.

The Old Cave   Finding a Talking Rock
The Day I Went to Mars   Sleeping for a Hundred Years

You can write stories about things that are make-believe.

Revising

Writing complete sentences

You probably know that a **complete sentence** begins with a capital letter and ends with a period, an exclamation point, or a question mark. But a complete sentence also tells a whole idea. A complete sentence tells at least one whole thought.

Read the complete sentence below.

subject ～ People walk. ～ verb

The short sentence above is a complete sentence because it has both a subject and a verb. A *subject* names the person or thing the sentence is about. You already know that a verb tells action. Every complete sentence has both a subject and a verb.

Look at the picture below.

A. Read the word groups on the next page that tell about the picture. Some of the word groups are complete sentences. But some of the word groups are not complete sentences. Decide which word groups are complete sentences and write **CS** next to them. Then write **NS** next to the word groups that are not complete sentences.

1. ___ Mr. Brownstein over there.

2. ___ Mr. Brownstein is funny.

3. ___ Mr. Brownstein dark hair.

4. ___ Mr. Brownstein does tricks.

5. ___ Mr. Brownstein yesterday.

B. Now write complete sentences of your own using the word groups below. Write one complete sentence for each word group that is given. One is done to show you how.

My favorite food *is roasted snake skin.* _____

1. The boy _____

2. All of Pam's friends _____

_____

3. The greatest trick _____

_____

4. The old worn-out car _____

_____

Copy the word groups below on another sheet of paper. Then, using each word group, write complete sentences.

1. The sleeping baby
2. Finally, Steve
3. Karen
4. The best thing about school
5. Watch out for

6. Then they
7. All of a sudden
8. Keep the
9. The kangaroo
10. After school we

Every complete sentence has both a subject and a verb.

Proofreading

Writing verbs that tell what already happened

Gillian's tooth ach**es.**
Gillian's tooth ach**ed** yesterday.

A. Read the sentences above. Then write answers to the questions on the lines below.

1. What are the verbs in the sentences?

   _____

2. Which sentence, the first or the second, tells what is hap-

   pening **now**? _____

3. Which sentence tells what has **already happened**?

   _____

You know that verbs have different forms to tell about singular subjects or plural subjects. Verbs also have different forms to tell **when** something happens. Most verbs end with **ed** when they tell about something that has *already happened*.

B. Read the pairs of sentences below. Then write the correct form of the verb on each line. One is done to show you how.

The old door <u>squeaks</u> now.

The old door <u>squeaked</u> yesterday.

1. He yells at the cow.

   He _____ at the cow yesterday.

2. She peeks in the door.

   She _____ in the door last night.

Some verbs *don't add* <u>ed</u> to tell about something that has already happened. Instead they change spelling. Read the sentences below. Notice how the verbs change spelling to tell about something that has already happened.

The children eat ice cream.
The children **ate** ice cream.
I see the ball.
I **saw** the ball.

Other verbs that change spelling to tell what already happened are: *feel—felt, run—ran, fly—flew, take—took, catch—caught, drink—drank, throw—threw*. If you are not sure of how a verb is spelled, look it up in your dictionary.

C. Read the sentences below. Then write the correct verb form that tells about what already happened. One is done to show you how.

They take five minutes.

They ___*took*___ five minutes.

1. I feel great.

   I_____great.
2. We drink ice tea.

   We_____ice tea.
3. I take a walk in the afternoon.

   I_____a walk in the afternoon.

Most verbs end with <u>ed</u> to tell if something already happened. Some verbs change spelling to tell if something already happened.

Post-Test

1. Write the word <u>fact</u> beside the sentences that are facts. Write the word <u>false</u> beside the sentences that are not true. Write <u>opinion</u> beside the sentences that are opinions.

   a. _____ Football is the best sport of all.

   b. _____ Each child in my class is 30 feet tall.

   c. _____ Texas is a state of the United States.

   d. _____ You should stand on your head every night.

2. Write **CS** beside each word group that is a complete sentence. Write **NS** beside each word group that is not a complete sentence.

   a. _____ They outside.   c. _____ Running around.

   b. _____ Pat came.   d. _____ It was there.

3. Write the word <u>now</u> next to each verb that you would use to tell what is happening now. Write the word <u>past</u> next to each verb that you would use to tell what already happened.

   a. _____ takes   c. _____ tell

   b. _____ threw   d. _____ walked

4. On a separate piece of paper, write a paragraph that tells what you like about your own town or neighborhood. Begin with three sentences that give only facts. Then write two sentences that give your opinions.

unit 6
Writing About Cause and Effect

Things to Remember When Writing About Cause and Effect

A **cause** is what makes something happen. An **effect** is what happens.

Writing

- Use words like *since*, *so*, and *because* to join cause and effect parts of sentences.
- Use causes and effects in paragraphs that explain how things work or how something happens.

Revising

- Combine sentences that have the same subjects or verbs to make your writing smoother.

Proofreading

Check to see that you have
- used an apostrophe to show ownership
- used an apostrophe to join words such as *has* and *not*
- used a comma between names of cities and states
- used a comma between a day and a year
- used a comma after a greeting in a letter
- used a comma after a closing in a letter

Writing about cause and effect in pictures

Look at the two pictures below.

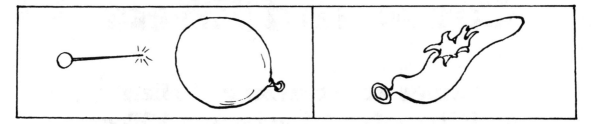

A **cause** is what makes something happen. What is the cause in

the pictures? Write your answer on the line. _____

_____

An **effect** is what happens as a result of a cause. What is the ef-

fect in the pictures? _____

A. Look at the pictures below and on the next page. Match each
picture under the word **Cause** with a picture under the word
Effect. Draw a line between the cause and effect pictures to
show which pictures should match.

Cause	Effect
1. 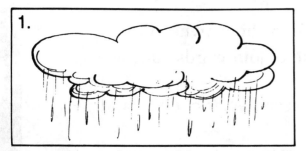	a. 
2. 	b. 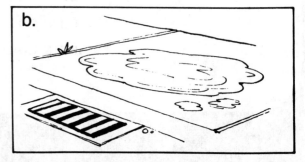

3.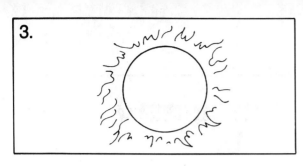

c.

4.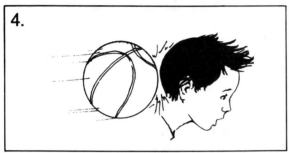

d.

B. Look at the next picture. What is about to happen? Draw a picture of the effect. Or write a sentence that describes the effect. Remember, the effect is what happens after the cause. Write your sentence on the line below. Draw your picture in the space.

The effect is: _____

On a separate sheet of paper write five cause and effect sentences. Just think of things that happen every day. One is done to show you how.

Cause: The <u>cause</u> is pushing the light switch.

Effect: The <u>effect</u> is the light coming on.

A cause is what makes something happen.
An effect is what happens as a result of a cause.

2 Writing with cause and effect words

Certain words or groups of words can join the cause and effect parts of a sentence. Read the sentences below. Notice the words that join the cause and effect parts.

I bought Donald a present **because** it was his birthday.
The tar in the street was melting **as a result of** the hot weather.

A. Write answers to the following questions on the lines.

1. What is the cause in the first sentence?

   _____

2. What is the effect in the first sentence?

   _____

3. What is the cause in the second sentence?

   _____

4. What is the effect in the second sentence?

   _____

5. What are the words that join the cause and effect parts of both sentences?

   _____   _____

Some other words and groups of words that can join the cause and effect parts of a sentence are *so, since, on account of, due to the fact that.*

B. Underline the word or words that join the cause and effect parts in the sentences below.

1. I told Ellen to come home because it was time for dinner.
2. My brother and I have saved ten dollars as a result of putting twenty cents in our bank every week.
3. The school was closed yesterday on account of the snowy weather.
4. Sarah could not go to the party due to the fact that she was sick with a bad cold.

C. Write a cause and effect ending for each sentence below. Use a word or word group that will join the cause and effect parts of your sentences.

1. I had to wear boots to school _____

   _____

2. I like you _____

   _____

3. Albert had to stay after school _____

   _____

4. We are going to have a party _____

   _____

 On a separate sheet of paper write four cause and effect sentences of your own. Be sure to use words or word groups that join the cause and effect parts in each of your sentences. If you need help, look back at part **B** of this lesson.

Use words like <u>because</u>, <u>since</u>, and <u>on account of</u> to join cause and effect parts of sentences.

---

3 Writing cause and effect sentences

A sentence that tells about a cause is often followed by a sentence that tells about an effect. Or a sentence that tells about an effect may come first. In either case, sentences of cause and effect are related.

A. Read the next two sentences.

The careless elephant stepped on my big toe. I wore a cast on my foot for six months.

Which sentence tells the cause? _____

Which sentence tells the effect? _____

B. Read the cause and effect sentences below. Then match each cause sentence to an effect. Draw lines between the sentences to show which ones should be matched.

Cause Sentences	**Effect Sentences**
1. Oliver stood on his head.	a. Mother painted the kitchen orange.
2. It was my ninth birthday.	b. Toni raced to the door.
3. Someone was ringing the doorbell.	c. The turkey in the oven was almost done.
4. I wish I were sixteen.	d. Suddenly he toppled over.
5. It needed a coat of paint.	e. My sister gave me a present.
	f. Then I could drive a car.

C. Now read the sentences below that tell causes. Then write sentences below each one to tell a related effect. One is done to show you how.

It was a wonderful program.

We clapped and whistled.

1. Yesterday was my birthday.

_____

2. I slammed the door.

_____

3. Elmo helped his father clean the windows.

_____

D. The following sentences tell effects. Write a sentence above each one to tell a related cause.

_____

1. My dog barked and licked my hand.

_____

2. I could not get up in the morning.

_____

3. So there was an awful noise.

On another sheet of paper, write a paragraph of at least 5 sentences. Write about something you would like to happen. Tell what could *cause* your wish to happen. You may use one of the ideas below or you may think up your own idea.

To live on the moon   To be in the Olympics
To be a great singer   To run for President

_____
Cause and effect sentences often go together in a paragraph.

Writing paragraphs that explain

Many things that happen can be **explained**. Explaining means telling how something happens or how something works. For example, in the last lesson you explained effects by telling about causes.

Read the next paragraph that explains a computer.

A computer is a machine that solves problems very quickly by counting special numbers. Computers add, subtract, multiply, and divide. An operator "feeds" the computer special information and then tells the computer what to do by writing a program for it. By using a great many small *electronic* machines, computers can do a very large amount of work in a very short time.

A. Paragraphs that explain tell causes and effects. Underline the sentence that tells who causes the computer to work. Then circle one sentence that tells about an effect of a computer.

B. Write sentences that explain each item below. First tell what the item is. Then tell how it works. Use cause and effect sentences.

1. A door _____

_____

_____

_____

2. A bicycle _____

_____

_____

_____

 On another sheet of paper, write a paragraph that explains one of the items below. Or you may think up your own item to explain. Make sure your paragraph tells the following things: what the item is or does, what causes the item to work or be, what effects the item has. Make your paragraph at least five sentences long.

    A railroad train   A school
    Scissors   A pencil

Paragraphs that explain tell how something happens or works.

Writing story problems and endings

Do you think that Barry and Craig have a problem? They decided to paint the living room of Craig's house. But things got out of hand. The painting job was more difficult than they thought.

The picture can be the beginning of a story. It shows a problem. It can end by **solving** the problem. Solving a problem means telling how a problem is worked out.

A. Look at the picture again. Then choose the ending at the top of page 91 that solves the problem. Write an X beside the ending that you think is the best.

_____ Craig's father came home. Then the boys had to spend all day Saturday cleaning the paint off the walls.

_____ When Barry saw Craig's father come home, he hid in the closet. Then Craig's father punished Craig, and Barry sneaked out the back door.

_____ The boys were given a prize by Craig's father. Then they started their own house painting business.

B. Read the story *ending* below. Then write an **X** beside the story problem that you think the ending solves.

The men decided to place a board across the pit and walk over it. All but one of them made it. It had been an awful trip.

Story Problem 1. _____   Debby had to practice for two months to get ready for the race. On the day before the race she broke her ankle.

Story Problem 2. _____   There were only two openings out of the cave. One opening was blocked by fallen rock. The other was over a pit of giant spiders.

Story Problem 3. _____   Terry saw her cousin Dena, sleepwalking. Terry was about to wake Dena when suddenly she heard a crash.

Now write your own story on another sheet of paper. Begin your story with a story problem. Then solve your story problem with an ending. You may use one of the ideas below or you may think up your own idea.

Alone in a Forest   The Leaky Roof   Earning Money

You can write a story with a problem. Then solve the problem by telling how it is worked out.

Revising

Writing combined sentences

Read the next pair of sentences.

> Sheila watched the parade.
> Brenda watched the parade.

The sentence below **combines** the pair of sentences. *Combine* means "join."

> Sheila **and** Brenda watched the parade.

Read the next pair of sentences.

> Pete cooked the dinner.
> Pete washed the dishes.

The next sentence combines that pair of sentences.

> Pete cooked the dinner **and** washed the dishes.

Sometimes the *subjects* of sentences can be combined, and sometimes the *verbs* of sentences can be combined.

A. Write <u>one</u> combined sentence for each pair of sentences below and on the next page. Two have been done to show you how.

My hands are cold.
My feet are cold.   *My hands and feet are cold.*

Ursula went home.
Ursula went to bed.   *Ursula went home and went to bed.*

1. Sandy left at noon.
   Anne left at noon.

   _____

   _____

2. Angela hid behind the
   door.
   Malvia hid behind the
   door.

   _____

   _____

3. Seth reads a lot.
   Seth gets good grades.   _____

   _____

4. Charles speaks well.
   Charles writes well.   _____

   _____

5. The horse ran.
   The rabbit ran.   _____

   _____

Now look back at eight or more sentences that you have written for this unit. Combine the eight sentences into *four* sentences. Write your combined sentences on a separate sheet of
paper. If you can't find all eight sentences to combine, use the
sentences below.

1. Sadie works hard.   2. The tables are broken.
   Sadie plays hard.   The chairs are broken.
3. His hands are big.   4. The basketball team won.
   His feet are big.   The hockey team won.

**You can combine sentences that have the same subjects or the
same verbs. Combined sentences make your writing smoother.**

Read the letter below.

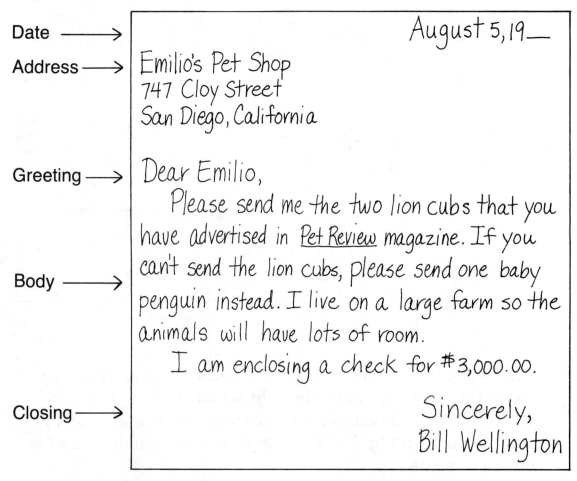

Date ⟶ August 5, 19___

Address ⟶ Emilio's Pet Shop
747 Cloy Street
San Diego, California

Greeting ⟶ Dear Emilio,

Body ⟶   Please send me the two lion cubs that you have advertised in <u>Pet Review</u> magazine. If you can't send the lion cubs, please send one baby penguin instead. I live on a large farm so the animals will have lots of room.
    I am enclosing a check for #3,000.00.

Closing ⟶ Sincerely,
Bill Wellington

Find this mark (,) and this mark (') in the letter. The *lower* mark is a **comma**. The *higher* mark is an **apostrophe**.

A. Now write answers to the following questions.

1. Between which two numerals is the comma placed in the date? ___ ___ This comma separates the day and the month from the year.

2. Between which two letters is an apostrophe placed in the

address? ____ ____ This apostrophe shows *ownership*. It shows that Emilio owns the pet shop.

3. Between which two words is a comma placed in the

    address? _____ _____ This comma separates the town from the state.

4. The comma in the greeting comes _____.

5. The comma in the closing comes _____.

An apostrophe is placed in the body of the letter in the word *can't*. This apostrophe does not show ownership like the apostrophe in the word *Emilio's*. Instead, it shortens two words to make one. The two words it shortens are the words *can* and *not*. Other words that can be shortened with an apostrophe are:

did and *not* — *didn't*   *was* and *not* — *wasn't*
has and *not* — *hasn't*   *could* and *not* — *couldn't*

B. Now write commas and apostrophes in the correct places for the sentences or word groups below.

1. We landed on April 5 1902.

2. He fed Arnold s shoes to the gorilla.

3. I can t see from way back here.

4. Dear Cousin Melissa

5. Sincerely yours George Flint

Use an apostrophe to show ownership.
Use an apostrophe to join two words.
Use a comma:
    between names of cities and states
    between the day and the year
    after a greeting
    after a closing

Post-Test

1. Circle the word or words that join cause and effect sentences.

   very fast   gently   yesterday
   because   as a result of   good-bye
   so   in the road   since

2. Write the letter of each effect next to its cause.

Causes		Effects
_____ The alarm clock rang.	a.	The cars stopped.
_____ The light turned red.	b.	The house got warm.
_____ Mom built a fire.	c.	Betty woke up.

3. Write one combined sentence for each pair of sentences below.

   a. The boy sang. _____

      The girl sang. _____

   b. The crowd moaned. _____

      The crowd groaned. _____

4. Write commas and apostrophes where they belong in the sentences or word groups below.

   a. I don t live in Bangor Maine.   c. This isn t Roger s book.

   b. April 12 1976   d. Dear Uncle Joe

5. On another piece of paper, write a paragraph that explains one of the items below. Use cause and effect sentences to tell how the item works.

   a stop sign   a window   a postage stamp   a rubber band

unit 7

Making Your Point in Writing

Things to Remember About Making Your Point in Writing

The **purpose** of a piece of writing may be to make people happy, to give facts, or to get people to do something.

Writing

- Think about your purpose before you start writing.
- Make your writing fit your purpose by adding details and sequence words.
- Tell who, what, when, where, and how much in announcements.
- Use plus or minus words when you write to get people to do something.

Revising

- Make all your verbs tell about the same time in a story.

Proofreading

Check that the letters you write
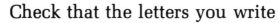
- have capital letters and commas where they are needed
- have a date in the heading
- have commas after the greeting and closing
- have greetings and closings that begin with capital letters

Writing for a purpose

The purpose of a jacket is to keep you warm. The purpose of a street sign is to tell you where you are. Almost everything has a purpose. Things people write usually have a purpose too.

A. Read the three items on the left below. Find each one's purpose on the right. Draw a line from each section of writing to its correct purpose.

1.

> **Hot Chocolate**
> 1 cup milk
> 1 tablespoon cocoa
> 1 marshmallow
>
> Heat milk in a pan. Put cocoa in cup. Pour hot milk into cup and stir. Put marshmallow on top and drink.

- A joke to make you laugh

2.

Al: Why does a cow wear a bell?
Sal: Her horns don't work.

- An ad to make you buy something

3.

> **Buy Aunt Sue's Moo Juice**
> It's the blueberry-flavored milk drink that will make you moo for more!

- A recipe telling you how to make something

There are three main purposes for writing. Stories and jokes are for people to enjoy. Recipes and directions give facts. Ads try to get people to do or buy something.

B. Now write something about apples. Choose a purpose for your writing. You may write a joke or story about apples. You may write an apple recipe or tell how to pick an apple. You may write an ad to get people to eat apples. Write your ideas on the lines below. Then write your purpose.

Purpose: _____

_____

On a separate sheet of paper, write three different things. Write a joke or story. Write a recipe or directions. Write an ad. Under each paragraph, write its purpose. Here are three ideas you can use if you wish.

    An elephant joke
    How to ride an elephant
    Why you should buy an elephant for a pet

Most writing is done for a purpose.

2 Writing to fit the purpose

a. Flasho Toothpaste brightens your smile. It has H3P05 to whiten teeth and freshen breath.

b. I once used Flasho Toothpaste. It was OK.

A. An ad should make you want to buy something. Read the two ads above.

1. Which ad makes you want to buy the toothpaste? _____

2. Which ad uses good-sounding words? _____

3. Can words help to sell things? _____

B. Directions should help you get somewhere. Read the two sets of directions below.

a. Take the Number 3 bus. Get off at Main Street. Walk right on Main for two blocks. The movie is on the corner of Main and Walnut Avenue.

b. Take a green bus. Get off near a park. Walk two blocks. You're at the movie.

1. Which set of directions would help you get to the movie?

   _____

2. Which set of directions has clear facts? _____

C. Stories should be fun to read. They should tell what happened clearly. Read this story that Tom wrote.

I had a funny dream. I went to a place. It was cold. I woke up without my blanket.

Can you make Tom's story fit the purpose better? Rewrite it, adding details and sequence words.

_____

_____

_____

_____

_____

_____

Write On Choose two items below. Write them on a separate sheet of paper.

1. Write an ad to sell a new food. Use good-sounding words.
2. Write directions to help someone get to your favorite park. Make your directions clear.
3. Write a story about a trip to the moon. Make it clear and fun to read.

When you write something, think about your purpose. Make your writing fit the purpose.

lesson

3 Writing a thank-you note

It is good to say thank-you when someone does something nice for you or gives you a present. One way to say thank-you is to write a note.

A. Maria liked the birthday present Uncle José gave her. She wrote this note.

> July 14, 19_
>
> Dear Uncle José,
>   The magic set you gave me is great. I practice with it every day after school. Now I can make a coin disappear. Soon I hope to make my brother disappear. Can you come over to see my magic show real soon?
>
>   Your niece,
>   Maria

Check the ways Maria lets her uncle know she likes his gift.

____ She says she likes it.

____ She tells how she uses it.

____ She says it isn't special.

____ She invites him to share the fun.

B. Maria wasn't as careful with the note she wrote to her cousin Reba. Here is her note.

> July 14, 19__
>
> Dear Reba,
>   I got the book on stars you sent me.
>   Your cousin,
>   Maria

How could Maria say thank-you to Reba in a better way? Look at the sentences you checked in **A.** Use some of those ideas to rewrite her note below.

Dear Reba,

_____

_____

_____

_____

_____

                Your cousin,
                Maria

 Think of someone you'd like to thank. Write that person a note on a separate sheet of paper. Here are some things you might thank someone for: driving you somewhere, making you something good to eat, telling you stories, being your friend.

A thank-you note thanks someone for a gift or favor. Your note should show that you are grateful to that person.

Writing an announcement

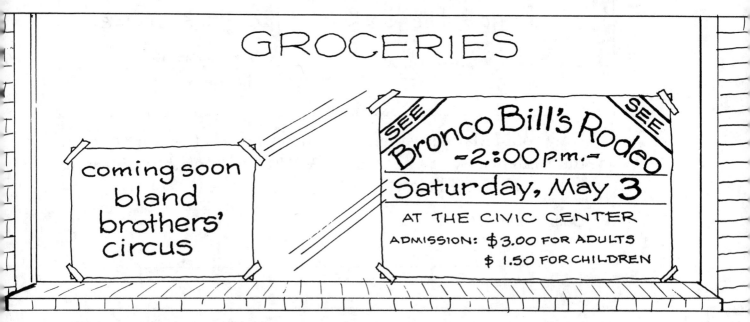

The purpose of an **announcement** is to tell about something that has happened or will happen soon. Announcements usually give information about who, what, where, when, and how much.

A. Look at the announcements in the store window above. Then answer the questions about them below.

1. Which announcement gives you more information — the one

   about the circus or the rodeo? _____

2. Fill in the blanks below. Copy the information from the announcement that gives it.

   Who or What? _____

   Where? _____

   When? _____

   How Much? _____

B. The picture below is of a movie that will soon open. Look at the picture and the information about the movie. Below the picture, write an announcement of the movie.

What: *Mouse on Mars*
Where: Rialto Theater
When: starts Wednesday, April 13
How Much: $2.50 for adults; $1.25 for children

_____

_____

_____

_____

_____

 Write an announcement for your next birthday. Decide if you would like to have a party or go someplace special. Draw a picture if you wish. Remember to tell who or what, when, and where.

Announcements tell who or what, when, where, and how much.

lesson 5 Writing an ad

The purpose of an ad is to get people to buy or do something. Ads do this in different ways. Some ads use **loaded words.** Plus-loaded words, like *wonderful* and *bright*, are good-sounding. Minus-loaded words, like *broken* and *sad*, are bad-sounding.

A. Next to each word below, put a + if it is plus-loaded. Put a − if it is minus-loaded.

____ fresh   ____ dull   ____ sparkle

____ dirty   ____ clean   ____ tired

Here is how loaded words can be used in an ad for a new soap.

Tired of dirty, dull skin? Use ZOWIE SOAP.
It will make you feel fresh and clean.
Famous star Marla Moore says,
"When I use ZOWIE, it makes my skin sparkle."

The ad above shows another way to try to make people buy something. An ad can say that a famous person uses the product.

B. Suppose you wanted to sell a new kind of sneaker or running shoe, called Swifty Shoe. Which words below would you use? Draw a circle around each.

tasty   sweet   fast   loser

comfortable   good-fitting   winner   chewy

C. Which person below would you use in your sneaker ad? Put an X next to that person's name.

_____ Homer Brown is a third-grader who wears sneakers.

_____ Pedro Lopez is a winning runner who wears sneakers.

_____ Violet Vocal is a singer who never wears sneakers.

D. Now write your ad for the Swifty Shoe. Use the words you picked in **B** and the person you picked in **C**.

_____

_____

_____

_____

_____

Pretend you just invented a new kind of toy or food. Think about what makes it special. List the loaded words you will use. Will you use a person in your ad? Then write an ad to sell your invention. Draw a picture if you wish.

Ads use loaded words and famous people to help sell things.

Revising

Writing verbs that agree

Read the next paragraph. Think about what is wrong with it.

I climb onto the space ship. It takes off. Soon we are streaking toward Planet Ultron. Then we landed with a bump.

What is wrong? The first three verbs tell the story as if it is happening now. They tell about present time. But in the last sentence, the verb is a past form. The last verb tells about past time. But the last verb should agree with the sentences in the rest of the story. The verb should be in present form. The sentence should say, "Then we land with a bump."

When you write a story, you can tell it with present time verbs or past time verbs. But don't change the time of the verbs in the middle of a story.

A. Read each paragraph below. Decide if the sentences tell about present or past time. Then underline the correct verb form to use for the last sentence in each paragraph.

1. The cat chased the mouse. The dog chased the cat. Grandpa (runs, ran) after the dog.
2. The frog raises his magic wand. He taps the princess. Suddenly she (turns, turned) into a frog.
3. Yoko looked out of the window sadly. It was raining again. Then her brother rushed into the room. He (carries, carried) a big box.

B. Now write your own story about a house. You can make it a ghost story or a funny story. The first sentence is started. You must underline the present or past verb form — whichever you want to use. Then write the rest of your story. Keep your verbs all in present or past time.

The old house (stands, stood) at the top of a dark hill.

_____

_____

_____

_____

_____

_____

 Look back over the **Write Ons** you've done for this unit. Find a story you wrote. Look at your verbs. Do they tell about the same time? Change any that don't. Then try rewriting the story to change the time. If it tells about present time, make it past. If it tells about past time, make it present.

Don't change the time of your verbs in the middle of a story.

Proofreading

Using good letter form

Here is a letter written in good form.

Heading ———→

June 8, 19___

Greeting ———→ Dear Burt,

Would you like to keep my pet snake for the summer? I can't take him to camp with me. His name is Sneaky. He likes to curl up in my pocket. Please let me know if you want him.

Body ———→

Closing ———→ Your friend,

Signature ———→ Ernie

A. Look carefully at the five parts of the letter above.
Then answer these questions.

1. What is in the heading? _____

2. Where do you see commas? _____

_____

3. Besides the first words of sentences, what words begin with capital letters? _____

_____

4. What part gives the writer's name? _____

B. On the lines below, write these letter parts in good form. Put them in the right places. Use capital letters and commas.

june 13, 19—
dear ernie
I'd love to take Sneaky. When can I get him?
your friend
burt

_____

_____

_____

_____

_____

_____

Use good form when you write a letter. Use capital letters and commas where they are needed. Remember these rules about writing letters:
The heading gives the date.
Commas come after the greeting and closing.
The greeting and closing begin with capital letters.

Post-Test

1. Write the purpose of each item below: to make you laugh; to make you buy something; to give directions.

   a. For amazing comfort and fun, buy Gilde-Alongs. The tiny jet engines in these sneakers mean you'll never have to walk again!

   _____

   b. Bill: What word is made shorter by adding two letters?
      Jill: Short!

   _____

2. | CAT SHOW AT ECHO PARK. APRIL 15. 2:00 P.M. |

   Use the information in the announcement to answer the questions.

   What? _____

   When? _____

   Where? _____

3. Put commas and capital letters in the letter below.

   june 3 19—

   dear uncle max

       Thank you for the records. I play them every day!

   your niece

   justine

4. Think of something that you own but don't ever use. If you wanted to sell it, what special plus-loaded words would you describe it with? List them. Then write a letter to a friend in which you try to persuade him or her to buy the object. Use good letter form.

unit 8

Point of View in Writing

Things to Remember About Point of View in Your Writing

A **point of view** is how someone sees and thinks about something.

Writing Tips
- Think about your point of view before you begin to write.
- Try writing about something from different points of view.
- Use different points of view for different characters in a story.

Revising and Proofreading Tips

Check to see that
- your words are exact and interesting
- your spelling, capital letters, punctuation marks, and verb forms are correct

Describing what you view

Can you guess what the pictures show? It is an ear of corn. The first picture shows how the corn looks to an ant. The second picture shows how the corn looks to a giraffe.

A. How does an ear of corn look to you? On the lines below, write a description of corn—growing in a field, or on your plate at dinner.

_____

_____

_____

_____

_____

Where you are can change the way you see something and write about it. Is it far away or close? Do you see only the top or the bottom? You can describe something differently, depending on how you view it.

B. Read each paragraph below about clouds. Under each, write who is viewing the clouds — a pilot in a plane or a person lying in the grass.

1. The clouds above look like puffy white animals. They change from elephants to fish to tigers as they march across the sky.

   I am _____.

2. I look down on the clouds. They are like a fluffy white rug under me.

   I am _____.

Try to describe something from two views. First, be yourself and tell how you see it. Then pretend you are an ant looking at it up close — maybe seeing only a small part. Or else pretend you are way up above it, looking down from a plane or a tall building. How does it look from far away? Under each paragraph, tell how you are viewing the thing. Here are some things you might choose to describe:

a flower or tree   a lake   a roller coaster

Where you are can change the way you see something and write about it.

2 Writing about feelings

A. It is starting to rain. Do all the people in the picture feel the same way about the rain? On the lines below, tell how you think they feel and why.

1. The children feel _____

_____

_____

_____

2. The woman feels _____

_____

_____

_____

    People can look at the same thing, like rain, differently. The way someone looks at, or views, something is called a **point of view.** Your point of view may come from where you stand. It may also come from the way you feel.

B. Have you ever waited in line to see a movie? Imagine that there is a long line waiting to see the latest hit. Write a sentence or two to describe how you think each of these people might be feeling. Use *I* when you write if you wish.

The first person in line: _____

_____

_____

_____

The last person in line: _____

_____

_____

_____

The ticket-seller: _____

_____

_____

_____

Write On   A telephone is something that you see and use every day. But think about it from a different point of view. Choose two of the people below. Write about a telephone as each one might view it. Use *I* when you write.

someone from Mars	a tired person trying to sleep
a telephone repairer	someone with good news to tell

People can have different points of view about the same thing. You can write about something from different points of view.

3 Writing about different characters

A **character** is a person in a story. The picture shows three characters about to go on a long space trip. They are Amanda, an astronaut;
Jimmy, a young boy; and Chris, a news reporter.

A. Read each paragraph that follows. Decide which character is
telling about the trip. Write the name of the character after the
paragraph that tells how he or she feels.

1. Wow! I've never been away from home before. Now I'm
   going into space. I hope I don't get homesick.

   _____

2. What a story this will make! I hope some exciting things
   happen, so I can write about them.

   _____

3. I've been training for this trip for a long time. I can't wait to practice what I've learned.

_____

B. Now suppose that the three travelers are in space. They see a strange spaceship heading toward them. How would each person act? Write a sentence or two next to each character. Tell what each one says or feels.

Amanda: _____

_____

_____

_____

Jimmy: _____

_____

_____

_____

Chris: _____

_____

_____

_____

Write On What might happen on the space trip? Will the spaceship crash? Will the travelers get to the moon or a planet? Write a short story about the trip. Tell what each person does and says.

_____

Different characters in a story act differently.

Writing a story from different views

Don is selling cookies to earn some extra money. He comes to the old Miller place, which people say is haunted. His friends dare him to ring the bell.

A. How do you think Don feels? Write the beginning of a story as if you were Don. Use *I* if you wish.

_____

_____

_____

_____

_____

_____

B. Boris, a mean-looking servant, opens the door. What does Don say and do? Write what happens next from Don's point of view.

_____

_____

_____

_____

_____

C. Tell how the story ends. What happens to Don?

_____

_____

_____

_____

_____

 Now tell the same story from a different point of view. Choose A or B to do on a separate sheet of paper.

A. Be Boris. How do you feel living in an old house that people are afraid of? What happens when Don rings the bell?

B. Be one of Don's friends. How do you feel when he takes your dare? What do you see and hear from behind the fence? What do you do?

You can write a story from one character's point of view. You can write about the same happenings from another character's point of view.

lesson 5

Rewriting

Two people went there. They saw some funny things. They enjoy it very much.

The story above doesn't tell very much. But you can make it more interesting when you rewrite it. You can use exact nouns and verbs. You can add adjectives to describe people and things. You can add adverbs to tell where, when, or how. You can combine sentences if you want to. You can check to see that all verbs tell about the same time.

A. Now rewrite the story at the top of the page. Make it as interesting as you can.

_____

_____

_____

_____

_____

Lorna wrote this paragraph about the circus. Her story is interesting, but she didn't proofread it.

Uncle willis and Gina went to the circas on saturday They seen a woman riding on elephant and lien jump through a hoop? One clown put on Ginas hat, but she didnt mind. gina and her uncle enjoyed the day, and they hopes to go again next year.

B. Proofread Lorna's story. Use proofreading marks and write in the corrections needed. Turn to page 14 if you need help.

Look back over the **Write Ons** you've written for this unit. Pick one to rewrite. First, choose words that make your story as interesting as you can. Then, proofread to be sure your spelling, capital letters, punctuation marks, and verb forms are correct. When you are happy with your **Write On,** copy it neatly.

When you finish writing, check to see that your words are exact and interesting. Then proofread your work to be sure that it's correct.

1. What is Raoul describing from his point of view?

   I am on the end of a long board. Terry is on the other end. The middle of the board is on top of a short post. When I touch the ground, Terry goes up in the air.

   Raoul is playing on a _____ .

2. Read each viewpoint about a spider web. Write the letter of each viewpoint beside the person or insect that would have it.

   a. Look at this beautiful
      spider web on our gate! ____ a tired old spider

   b. I get so tired spinning
      this web every night! ____ a person who sees a web

   c. Get me out of this awful
      web before it's too late! ____ a fly trapped in a web

3. Here are two story characters: Sly, a worm who lives in an apple, and Anna, a girl who starts to eat the apple. Write the name of the character who might say each line below.

   a. "Ugh! What are you doing in my apple!" _____

   b. "Your apple! I was here first!" _____

4. Pretend you are from a faraway planet and are visiting Earth for the first time. You do not know what any of the items below are. Write a paragraph that describes one of them for your friends and family back home.

   a traffic jam   a horse race   a football game

Answer Key

Unit 1

Lesson 1 (pages 2–3)

A. **Animals with Four Legs**
   camel   elephant   zebra
   Animals That Crawl
   ant   spider   snake
   Animals with Feathers
   parrot   peacock   ostrich
B. **Fruits**   **Colors**   **Holidays**
   grape, etc.   blue, etc.   Halloween, etc.
C. **Family Members**
   sister   mother   brother   ~~car~~
   Drinks
   lemonade   ~~cake~~   milk   water
   Parts of the Face
   cheek   nose   ~~foot~~   ear

Lesson 2 (pages 4–5)

A. 1. Some girls and boys are playing volleyball.
B. 3. Fred is cooking hamburgers.
C. ⇨ When you see this symbol, check with your teacher.

Lesson 3 (pages 6–7)

A. 2. Fish sleep differently.
B. 1. I rushed to go camping.
C. ⇨

Lesson 4 (pages 8–9)

A. 1. Tulips are my favorite flowers.
   2. We have to stand in rows at school.
   3. It doesn't tell about the main idea.
B. 1. Our neighbor took a trip into space.
   2. I took a trip to Disney World.
   3. Tugboats move large ships.
   4. I'd like to sail a ship someday.

Lesson 5 (pages 10–11)

A. 1. Monkey Is Star of Bike Day
B. 3. A Bad Beginning for Charlotte
C. You might say: UFO's—Real or Not?

Lesson 6 (pages 12–13)

A. The clown fed the elephant.
B. Answers will be different. You might say:
   2. eggs   banana
   3. doll   kite
   4. rose   daisy
C. ⇨

Lesson 7 (pages 14–15)

A. 1. s̶   2. g̶o̶   3. ∧
B. Bert loves to runs. He sometimes ^runs all day long. this
   ↗car ↗year he will be on the school ^track team.
C. ⇨

Unit 2

Lesson 1 (pages 18–19)

A. 1. first   last   next   2. next   first   last
B. Your picture should show the girl holding her unwrapped present.
C. You might say:
   First: Anne gets a present for her birthday.
   Next: Anne opens the package.
   Last: The (toy elephant, etc.) was just what she wanted!

Lesson 2 (pages 20–21)

A. 2 1 3   3 1 2
B. You should have underlined:
   First, Then, Finally
C. ⇨

Lesson 3 (pages 22–23)

A. First   Then   Next   Then   Finally   Now
B. **Things You Will Need**
   2 cups flour   1 teaspoon salt
   3 tablespoons water   2 eggs
   Things to Do
   First, break the eggs into the flour.
   Next, add the water and salt and stir.
   Finally, roll out the mixture.

Lesson 4 (pages 24–25)

A. The picture should be a star.
B. 6 2 4 5 3 1
C. ⇨

Lesson 5 (pages 26–27)

A. 1. beginning   end   middle
   2. middle   beginning   end
B. 1. end ⇨   2. middle ⇨   3. beginning ⇨

Lesson 6 (pages 28–29)

A. 1. danced   2. jumped   3. scurried
B. Answers will be different. You might say:
   2. stepped   marched   3. bit   chewed
   4. yelled   whispered
C. ⇨

Lesson 7 (pages 30–31)

A. 1. capital letter   2. capital letter
   3. J   H   4. capital letter

B. Michelle Myers goes to East Windsor School. She jogs down Spring Street and sprints over to Vine Street. Every Wednesday she has soccer practice. On those days, she rides over to Stanleyville.

Unit 3

Lesson 1 (pages 34–35)
A. 1. One player is thinner.
2. One animal is longer.
3. The boy and girl are the same height.
B. 2. The woman on the left is bigger. (or: The woman on the left is louder.)
3. The two dogs look the same.

Lesson 2 (pages 36–37)
A. You might have said:
The boat on the left is fancier (newer, longer).
The boat on the right is smaller (shorter).
B. ⇦

Lesson 3 (pages 38–39)
A. 1. more than two   2. two
3. more than two
B. ⇦   **C.** ⇦

Lesson 4 (pages 40–41)
A. 1. better   2. best   3. worse
4. worst
B. ⇦

Lesson 5 (pages 42–43)
A. 1. the wind   2. two   3. two
B. ⇦

Lesson 6 (pages 44–45)
A. You should have underlined:
1. huge, bright, new   2. tiny, clumsy, old
B. You should have underlined:
1. shiny blue   2. large   3. fluffy
4. soft, green
C. ⇦

Lesson 7 (pages 46–47)
A. 1. period   2. period
3. question mark   4. exclamation point
B. 1. How long is that boat?
2. Finish painting the fence by tomorrow.
3. Mr. Hernandez took us to the zoo.
4. Wow! Look at that hit!
5. Where are you going?
6. There is a crowd outside the palace. (or !)
7. Don't push! (or .)
8. Will the king give a speech?
C. ⇦

Unit 4

Lesson 1 (pages 50–51)
A. 1. R   2. L   3. R   4. R   5. L
B. ⇦

Lesson 2 (pages 52–53)
A. 1. smell   2. taste, seeing
B. apple

Lesson 3 (pages 54–55)
A. You should have circled: fluffy, soft, furry
You might have written: sleepy, white, or happy
B. ⇦

Lesson 4 (pages 56–57)
A.
short	tall
wearing glasses	thin
flowered dress	curly hair
long hair	dark hair
light hair	short hair
B. ⇦

Lesson 5 (pages 58–59)
A. 1. egg   2. teeth
B. 1. I bark.   2. People fly in me.

Lesson 6 (pages 60–61)
A. 1. quietly   2. outside   3. now
B. You should have underlined:
1. outside, today   2. happily
3. loudly   4. upstairs
5. Later, peacefully
C. ⇦

Lesson 7 (pages 62–63)
A. 1. gulps, gulp   2. one ends in *s*
3. gulp
B. You should have underlined:
1. walks   2. looks   3. smell
4. grow   5. shines
C. You should have underlined:
1. Play   2. Jumps   3. Eat
4. Climb
D. ⇦

Unit 5

Lesson 1 (pages 66–67)
A. T   O   O   F
B. 1. fact   2. false   3. opinion
4. fact   5. false
C. ⇦

Lesson 2 (pages 68–69)
A. ➥   B. ➥

Lesson 3 (pages 70–71)
A. **You should have underlined these sentences:**
I'm 8 years old.
I weigh 65 pounds and I am 4 feet tall.
I have green eyes and blond hair.
In the summer, I get millions of freckles.
Well, maybe I don't get millions, but I do get a lot.
That's when you go looking for caves.
I'll talk to you about a visit when I see you in school next week.
You should have circled these sentences:
I'm glad you just moved into our neighborhood.
I sure do enjoy meeting people my own age.
My favorite hobby is spelunking.
I think spelunking is a good hobby because it's so exciting.
My favorite school subject is math.
I enjoy math because it gives me a chance to figure out problems on my own.
I also like math because it is easy for me.
I would like to know more about you.
I hope we will become good friends.
B. ➥

Lesson 4 (pages 72–73)
A. ➥   B. ➥

Lesson 5 (pages 74–75)
A. 1. M   2. M   3. M   4. F
B. ➥

Lesson 6 (pages 76–77)
A. 1. NS   2. CS   3. NS   4. CS
   5. NS
B. ➥

Lesson 7 (pages 78–79)
A. 1. aches, ached   2. first   3. second
B. 1. yelled   2. peeked
C. 1. felt   2. drank   3. took

Unit 6

Lesson 1 (pages 82–83)
The pin is the cause. The broken balloon is the effect.
A. 1. b   2. a   3. d   4. c
B. You probably wrote or drew that the waiter slipped and dropped the tray.

Lesson 2 (pages 84–85)
A. 1. Donald's birthday   2. buying a present
   3. the hot weather   4. melting tar
   5. because   as a result of

B. 1. because   2. as a result of
   3. on account of   4. due to the fact that
C. ➥

Lesson 3 (pages 86–87)
A. first   second
B. 1. d   2. e   3. b   4. f   5. a
C. ➥   D. ➥

Lesson 4 (pages 88–89)
A. You should have underlined this sentence:
An operator "feeds" the computer special information and then tells the computer what to do by writing a program for it.
You should have circled any of the other sentences.
B. ➥

Lesson 5 (pages 90–91)
A. Craig's father came home. Then the boys had to spend all day Saturday cleaning the paint off the walls.
B. The X belongs next to Story Problem 2.

Lesson 6 (pages 92–93)
A. 1. Sandy and Anne left at noon.
   2. Angela and Malvia hid behind the door.
   3. Seth reads a lot and gets good grades.
   4. Charles speaks well and writes well.
   5. The horse and the rabbit ran.

Lesson 7 (pages 94–95)
A. 1. 5, 19—   2. o s
   3. San Diego, California
   4. After *Emilio*   after *Sincerely*
B. 1. We landed on April 5, 1902.
   2. He fed Arnold's shoes to the gorilla.
   3. I can't see from way back here.
   4. Dear Cousin Melissa,
   5. Sincerely yours, George Flint

Unit 7

Lesson 1 (pages 98–99)
A. 1. A recipe telling you how to make something
   2. A joke to make you laugh
   3. An ad to make you buy something
B. ➥

Lesson 2 (pages 100–101)
A. 1. a   2. a   3. yes
B. 1. a   2. a
C. ➥

Lesson 3 (pages 102–103)

A. You should have checked:
She says she likes it.
She tells how she uses it.
She invites him to share the fun.

B. ▷◁

Lesson 4 (pages 104–105)

A. 1. the rodeo
2. **Who or What?** Bronco Bill's Rodeo
Where? Civic Center
When? Saturday, May 3 at 2 P.M.
How Much? $3.00 for adults and $1.50 for children

B. ▷◁

Lesson 5 (pages 106–107)

A. + fresh   − dull   + sparkle
− dirty   + clean   − tired

B. You should have circled: comfortable, good-fitting, fast, winner (You might have circled *loser* if you wanted to use a minus-loaded word.)

C. You would probably choose Pedro Lopez.

D. ▷◁

Lesson 6 (pages 108–109)

A. 1. ran   2. turns   3. carried

B. ▷◁

Lesson 7 (pages 110–111)

A. 1. the date
2. in the date, after the greeting and closing
3. June, Dear, Burt, Sneaky, Your, Ernie
4. the signature

B.   June 13, 19--
Dear Ernie,
    I'd love to take Sneaky. When can I get him?
                    Your friend,
                    Burt

Lesson 1 (pages 114–115)

A. ▷◁

B. 1. a person lying in the grass
2. a pilot in a plane

Lesson 2 (pages 116–117)

A. You might have said something like this:
1. The children feel sad because the rain will spoil their picnic.
2. The woman feels happy because the rain will help her flowers grow and she won't have to water them.

B. ▷◁

Lesson 3 (pages 118–119)

A. 1. Jimmy   2. Chris   3. Amanda

B. ▷◁

Lesson 4 (pages 120–121)

A. ▷◁   B. ▷◁   C. ▷◁

Lesson 5 (pages 122–123)

A. ▷◁

B. Uncle Willis and Gina went to the circus on Saturday. They saw a woman riding on an elephant and a lion jump through a hoop. One clown put on Gina's hat, but she didn't mind. Gina and her uncle enjoyed the day, and they hope to go again next year.

Post-Test Answers; pg 16

1. Animals   Tools   Buildings
   car   butter tree
2. b
3. Answers will vary. Possible titles include: Wooden Bicycle Wheels; The First Bicycle Wheels; Riding on Wood; or some similar title.
4. Be sure the students have replaced the nouns *person* and *place* with more exact nouns. Check that the other sentences in the students' paragraphs support and develop the main idea of students' career plans. Look for any sentences that do not fit with this main idea.

Post-Test Answers; pg 32

1. a. 3 1 2
   b. 3 2 1
2. Answers will vary. Be sure that sequence words are used in proper order.
3. Answers will vary. Possible answers are:
   a. run, hop, walk, jump
   b. tap, pound, beat, strike
   c. pitch, toss, heave, scatter
   d. giggle, howl, chuckle, snicker
4. a. Next, Monday, Columbus Day, Lafayette School
   b. Last, May, Ellen Gray, I, Houston, Texas
5. Answers will vary. Check to see that the students have used sequence words to order the events. You might want to have the students underline the verbs in their sentences and decide whether they are exact enough.

Post-Test Answers; pg 48

1. a. softer   softest
   b. sweeter sweetest
   c. more interesting   most interesting
   d. more exciting   most exciting
2. a. better
   b. best
   c. worse
   d. worst
3. Answers will vary. Be sure that student similes compare unlike things.
4. Answers will vary. Accept any adjectives that sensibly modify the nouns in the titles. Be sure that each sentence develops the idea in the title. You might want to have the students underline the adjective(s) they used in their sentences.

Post-Test Answers; pg 64

1. Answers will vary. Possible details:
   a. A horse is running down the sidewalk.
   b. Two men with a lasso are chasing it.
   c. Four children are watching the horse.
   d. The horse trailer is blocking traffic.
   Accept any detail in the illustration.
2. bed
3. Answers will vary. Some possibilities are *yellow, delicious, soft, tasty, sweet*
4. Answers will vary. Some possibilities are:
   a. *fast, wildly, away, far, there, rapidly*
   b. *quickly, closely, nervously, now*
5. Answers will vary. You may suggest that the students write a title for their paragraph. Also ask them to underline the adverb(s) they have used in their sentences. Besides adverbs, look for adjectives and phrases that add details to the story.

Post-Test Answers; pg 80

1. a. opinion
   b. false
   c. fact
   d. opinion
2. a. NS   c. NS
   b. CS   d. CS
3. a. now   c. now
   b. past   d. past
4. Check to see that each student has written three sentences of fact and two sentences of opinion. Make sure each sentence keeps to the topic of good things about my town. You may want to ask the students to underline the words in the opinion sentences that indicate they are opinions. Students should also check their sentences to make sure they are complete.

Post-Test Answers; pg 96

1. because, so, as a result of, since
2. c, a, b
3. a. The boy and girl sang.
   b. The crowd moaned and groaned.
4. a. I don't live in Bangor, Maine.
   b. April 12, 1976.
   c. This isn't Roger's book.
   d. Dear Uncle Joe,
5. Check to make sure that the students have provided a definition of the item, an explanation of how it works, and a description of how it is used. You might want the students to underline any cause and effect words or phrases they have used.

Post-Test Answers; pg 112

1. a. to make you buy something
   b. to make you laugh
2. What? a cat show
   When? April 15 at 2:00 P.M.
   Where? Echo Park
3.
                       June 3, 19—
   Dear Uncle Max,
       Thank you for the records. I play them every day!
                       Your niece,
                       Justine
4. Check the students' letters for good letter form. Also check to make sure that students have used plus-loaded words to describe their objects.

Post-Test Answers; pg 124

1. see-saw
2. b, a, c
3. a. Anna
   b. Sly
4. Check to see that the paragraph is written from the point of view of an alien who is unfamiliar with the situations listed in the question. The paragraph should contain no specialized vocabulary associated with these situations, for example. You might want to have the students write a title for their paragraphs.